SUNDAY SUPPERS

SUNDAY SUPPERS

RECIPES + GATHERINGS

KAREN MORDECHAI

CLARKSON POTTER/PUBLISHERS
NEW YORK

Library of Congress Cataloging-in-Publication Data
Mordechai, Karen.
Sunday suppers / Karen Mordechai. -- First edition.
pages cm
1. Suppers. 2. Sunday. I. Title.
TX738.M67 2014
641.5'3—dc23   2013038842

ISBN 978-0-385-34526-2
Ebook ISBN 978-0-385-34527-9

Printed in China

Cover design by Rae Ann Spitzenberger
Cover photograph (inset): Karen Mordechai
Cover photograph (background): Shutterstock © photocell

10 9 8 7 6 5 4 3

First Edition

CONTENTS

Dining with one's friends and beloved family is certainly one of life's primal and most innocent delights, one that is both soul-satisfying and eternal.

—JULIA CHILD

INTRODUCTION

This book is a collection of small gatherings and meals across the country, in homes and in unexpected locales. You'll find recipes and inspiration for opening your homes or venturing outdoors with your loved ones. I hope that you will embrace new environments and bring care and joy to the meals shared.

Sunday Suppers is a communal cooking center and food website based out of Brooklyn, New York, whose premise is to bring together food, gatherings, and community. Through inspiration and instruction, Sunday Suppers allows people to gather and cook in their homes, and experience the world's oldest act of community: sharing a meal. At our suppers we remove much of the fuss and formality of "entertaining." The table is set in a modest manner, and the food is honest and straightforward. The focus is on a sense of togetherness and tradition that is richly formed and celebrated through these shared meals. We invite family, friends, and guests to join us in the preparation of the meals and to dine at our table. Strangers attend our dinners from across the globe and together a community has formed.

The idea for Sunday Suppers began in the spring of 2009 as an opportunity to cook and dine communally with friends in our loft home in Brooklyn. The intention was to create a beautiful cooking environment and bring back the nostalgia of family meals and early suppers with friends.

As an artist (and a tried-and true-Libra), I found myself torn between the balance of creation and capture. I was greatly influenced by the classic greats of street photography, such as Robert Frank and Eugene Smith, and was challenged to capture the city I lived in and the elusiveness of a moment. I also spent great time in my mother's and grandmother's kitchens, watching and documenting their cooking over the years.

As I continued to explore these concepts, I developed a yearning for the opportunity to marry the creation of beauty with the capture of it. Starting Sunday Suppers was a resolution of this need. I found I was able to cook, travel, create, and capture all at once. I began to create communal meals, like those I grew up with—but with a new slant. These gatherings would be joyful and of mixed crowds. These meals would be early suppers and, through cooking and learning, bonds would be formed. We would source local and sustainable fare, and together we would cook excellent food.

My husband and I held our first dinner at our home in Brooklyn. We moved our furniture into the back bedroom to make way for a long dining table. We cooked a meal with ten of our friends, sat down to eat, and had a lovely time. As the sun set over the water, we all toasted the meal and everything felt just right. The mood was casual and spirited, and the feeling of achievement filled the room.

Word about that first supper spread quickly—clearly something had resonated. Readers of my blog began writing in, asking to attend our next dinner, and so the story of Sunday Suppers began. Each meal became an opportunity to create a lovely setting and an inspired menu. The most exciting part was that a community had formed both online and in person. We began to work with amazing talents, such as guest chefs, artisans, and crafters. The growth and sense of collaboration has been exhilarating. We've recently opened a new home for Sunday Suppers: a large industrial loft that serves as a communal cooking and dining space where we host many meals. Our hopes are to expand and create hubs in other locations.

This book is an extension of our suppers, as it is in its essence a compilation of recipes that one might use to plan gatherings for groups both large and small. I hope this book inspires you to set out and make beautiful meals with the people you hold dear. Some menus involve more work, and others are easier to achieve. Take pieces from menus if you would rather not create the entire meal, and feel free to mix and match from one menu to the next. Draw ideas from the table settings and ingredients. Read this book before you head to the market for inspiration or curl up with it on the couch. I've also compiled a source guide (see page 250) in which I disclose my favorite shops for groceries, tableware, and other items for your gatherings.

Our food is not overly demanding fare; it is good, wholesome, and fairly approachable. Most of the ingredients should be readily available in local grocers or online specialty shops. The menus are straightforward and include classics like fries, paella, and ice cream. The novelty is in the subtle changes, the tweaks and nuances we often give to an otherwise expected menu. There's a pleasant surprise in finding Tea and Ginger–Cured Sea Bass (page 47) with Whipped Cream Cheese (page 45) on a brunch table, or Pickled Grapes (page 81) for a picnic to add an unexpected flavor.

Of paramount importance is the quality and integrity of ingredients. At Sunday Suppers, we source farm-fresh and local ingredients when possible and encourage you to do so as well. We especially like to support our local shops, artisans, and butchers as much as possible. By doing this, we have extended our sense of family and support and feel fortunate to have become part of an incredible community of folks.

And those who have attended one of our suppers know that the atmosphere is key. Here, too, we do not go overboard: less is more, as they say. While our decor is simple enough to follow, it is well thought out. We favor neutrals and handwritten notes. Small crafts and unexpected gifts are treats offered to attendees and are a wonderful way to bid farewell to your guests.

In this collection of stories I hope to bring a bit of joy and inspiration to you—to offer ideas while simultaneously imparting a sense of freedom to break the rules a bit and just do what feels right and beautiful to your eye.

MORNING

BREAKFAST FOR ONE, LOVINGLY PREPARED AND SERVED bedside—there is no greater treat. The envelope is hand-addressed in crayon with a love note tucked inside. A gift is wrapped in white paper and adorned with a few twigs we gathered from the yard. We light a fire and linger in bed a little bit longer.

MENU

CREAM BISCUITS WITH JAM BUTTERS

PERFECTLY SCRAMBLED EGGS

GREENS

BLOOD ORANGE, HALVED

GREEN JUICE

FRENCH PRESS COFFEE

This meal is simple yet delicious. The eggs are so
soft, they will remind you of Paris. This is my favorite
way to celebrate with a loved one.

Eldred, New York

CREAM BISCUITS WITH JAM BUTTERS

MAKES 8 BISCUITS

With a short ingredients list, this is the most achievable morning biscuit. And if you want to give yourself a head start, you can combine the dry ingredients the evening before, in the morning simply add the cream. This recipe will yield a few extra biscuits for the cook and perhaps for leftovers the next morning.

2 cups all-purpose flour, sifted, plus extra for dusting

2½ tablespoons sugar

2 teaspoons baking powder

½ teaspoon salt

1¾ cups heavy cream

Jam Butters, for serving (recipe follows)

Set an oven rack in the upper-middle position and preheat the oven to 350°F. Line a baking sheet with parchment paper.

In a large bowl, whisk together the flour, sugar, baking powder, and salt. Stir in the cream with a wooden spoon, mixing until a dough forms, about 30 seconds. Turn the dough out onto a lightly floured surface and gather it into a ball. Knead the dough until smooth, about 30 seconds.

Pat the dough to form a ¾-inch-thick round. Cut out 8 biscuits using a 2½-inch biscuit cutter, dipping the cutter in flour to keep the dough from sticking to it. (Do not twist the cutter; simply cut and lift.) Place the biscuits on the prepared baking sheet, and bake until golden brown, 12 to 15 minutes. Let the biscuits cool slightly on the baking sheet, and serve with the Jam Butters.

JAM BUTTERS

MAKES ½ CUP OF EACH FLAVOR

1½ cups (3 sticks) unsalted butter, at room temperature

3 tablespoons *each* of strawberry, apricot, and blueberry jams

By hand or with an electric mixer, in separate bowls, mix a stick of butter with each type of jam. Scrape into separate ramekins for serving, or place onto sheets of wax paper and roll into logs for storing. These will keep for a week in the refrigerator.

PERFECTLY SCRAMBLED EGGS

SERVES 1

This scramble is perfectly soft and fluffy with the added decadence of butter and cream. Use top-quality eggs here—farm-fresh if possible.

2 large free-range eggs

1 tablespoon heavy cream

½ teaspoon salt

1 tablespoon salted butter

Freshly ground black pepper to taste

In a small bowl, whisk together the eggs, cream, and salt.

Heat a medium skillet over low heat, and melt the butter in it. Lower the heat to very low, add the eggs, and scramble constantly, using a wooden spoon, for about 10 minutes. Remove the eggs from the heat while they are still custardy but not runny. (They will continue to cook once removed from the heat.) Top with pepper, and serve.

GREENS

SERVES 1

Use fresh market greens for this breakfast side: kale, spinach, chard, or collards all work nicely.

1 tablespoon olive oil

1 clove garlic, minced

1 cup chopped Lacinato kale

1 tablespoon water

Salt and freshly ground black pepper to taste

Heat the olive oil in a small skillet over low heat. Add the garlic and kale and cook, tossing frequently, until the greens begin to soften, about 5 minutes. Add the water and continue to cook for 2 more minutes. Season with salt and pepper. Serve warm.

GREEN JUICE

SERVES 1

Green, fresh, and subtly sweet, this juice includes olive oil and lemon juice to up the ante. We juice daily at the studio and find it to be a light, clean way to kick off the day.

3 kale leaves

1 apple

½ large English cucumber

Juice of ½ lemon

1 tablespoon olive oil

Press the kale, apple, and cucumber through a juice machine. Stir in the lemon juice and olive oil, and serve.

COOK'S NOTE | *If you do not have a juicer, use a blender. Core the apple, and blend all the ingredients on high speed. Strain the juice into a glass through a piece of cheesecloth or a fine-mesh sieve.*

|TAKE-ALONG

WE ARRIVE EARLY ON A CHILLY SPRING MORNING and watch the crowds trickle in—families and friends set up their stations for the day. We take photos and hike up trails. As morning turns to noon, we slowly make our way back, bringing home rocks and pebbles as tokens.

MENU

BREAKFAST BREAD

GRANOLA AND YOGURT

CINNAMON ICED COFFEE
AND CREAM

This meal is decidedly straightforward and easy to transport.
The breakfast bread is a fun play on an egg sandwich,
topped with bacon, egg, and cheese. Cinnamon iced coffee,
granola, and yogurt are packed in a beach bag.

Rodeo Beach, San Francisco

BREAKFAST BREAD

SERVES 4

This bread is a classic combination of flavors packed in a slightly more utilitarian form. You could certainly expand on the ingredients here—asparagus, mushrooms, and tomatoes would all work quite well. For transport, cut the bread into squares or simply bring along the pan.

1¼ teaspoons active dry yeast

1 teaspoon sugar

⅔ cup warm water (105°F)

1¾ cups all-purpose flour, plus extra for dusting

1 tablespoon milk powder

1½ teaspoons salt, plus extra for seasoning

2 tablespoons olive oil, plus extra for the bowl and for drizzling

4 strips bacon

4 to 6 large eggs

Freshly ground black pepper

¼ red onion, chopped into large pieces

1 cup shredded Gruyère cheese

Leaves from 3 sprigs fresh thyme

½ bunch fresh chives, chopped, for garnish

Combine the yeast, sugar, and warm water in a small bowl, and set aside in a warm place for 5 minutes, until bubbles form.

Combine the flour, milk powder, and salt in a large bowl. Add the yeast mixture and the olive oil. Knead in the bowl for 5 minutes. Transfer to an oiled bowl, cover, and allow to rest in a warm place for 1 to 1½ hours, until the dough has doubled in size.

Preheat the oven to 425°F. Line a 9 × 12-inch baking dish with parchment paper.

Heat a skillet over medium-high heat, add the bacon, and cook for about 1 minute on each side, until partially cooked. Set aside.

Roll the dough out on a floured surface and then transfer it to the prepared baking dish, stretching it to fit into the corners. Make four to six indentations in the dough, and crack an egg into each one. Season each egg with salt and pepper to taste. Arrange the onion pieces and bacon strips over the bread. Sprinkle with the cheese and thyme leaves and drizzle with olive oil.

Bake for 20 to 25 minutes, until the top is golden brown, the bacon is crisp, and the egg whites are set. Top with the chives.

GRANOLA

SERVES 10 TO 12

Some recipes age well over time as you tweak them again and again. This one has been tested and retested in our home. The granola breaks perfectly into crisp chunks with just the right bite of sweet and salt. We recommend you serve this with a creamy sheep's-milk yogurt.

¾ cup vegetable oil

⅓ cup honey

¼ cup granulated sugar

1 tablespoon light brown sugar

1 tablespoon vanilla extract

Pinch of sea salt

5 cups old-fashioned rolled oats

1 cup chopped almonds

1 cup chopped walnuts

1 cup dried cranberries or dried cherries

Preheat the oven to 325°F. Line a 13 × 17-inch rimmed baking sheet with parchment paper.

In a large bowl, thoroughly whisk together the oil, honey, both sugars, vanilla, and salt. Add the oats and nuts, and combine well. Pour the mixture onto the prepared baking sheet, patting it down to create a compact, even layer that fills the entire sheet.

Bake for 30 to 35 minutes, until golden brown, rotating the pan once midway through. Remove from the oven and allow the granola to rest, untouched, for 30 minutes. Then break the granola into chunks and add the cranberries or cherries. Stored in an airtight jar, it will keep for about 3 weeks.

CINNAMON ICED COFFEE AND CREAM

MAKES 3 TO 4 CUPS

Adding a little spice to your coffee is a neat trick; it makes it taste just a bit fancier. A sprinkle of cinnamon and a good full-bodied roast go a long way.

½ cup coffee beans, medium coarsely ground

¾ teaspoon ground cinnamon

4 cups boiling water

1 cinnamon stick

Ice cubes, for serving

Heavy cream, for serving

Place the ground coffee and the cinnamon in a 16-ounce French press coffee pot. Add the boiling water, stir, cover, and allow the coffee to steep for 4 minutes. Then insert the plunger and push it down. Transfer the coffee to a pitcher and add the cinnamon stick. Allow to cool before transporting in a thermos, or refrigerate overnight. Serve over ice in glasses or glass jars, adding cream to taste.

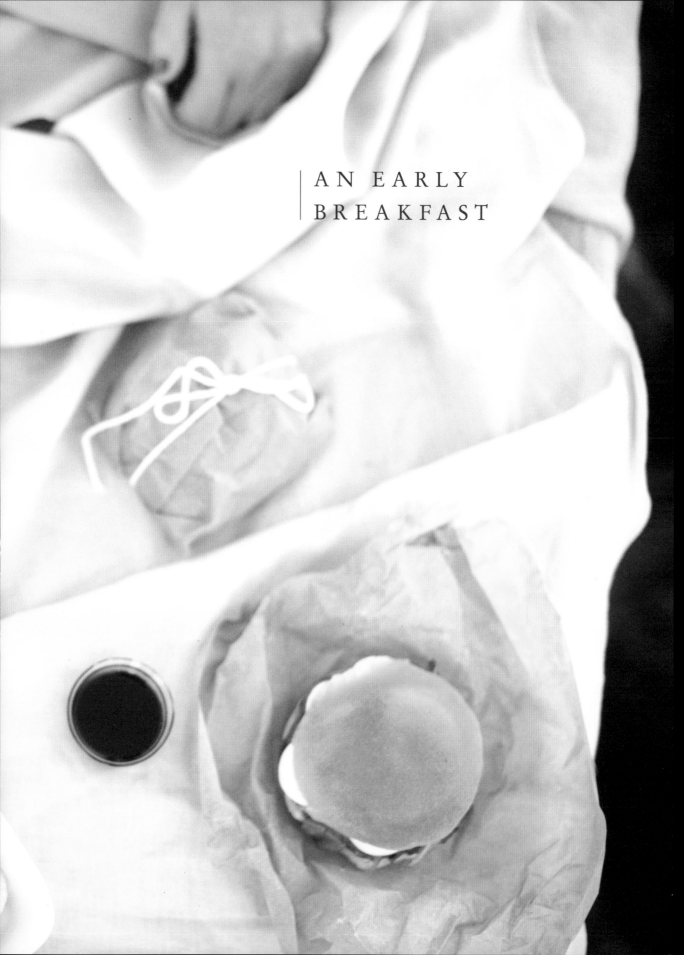

AN EARLY
BREAKFAST

THERE IS SOMETHING QUIETLY SACRED about early mornings in the city. The gestures of city-dwellers are a bit slower; the city hasn't quite woken up yet. Shopkeepers open their doors and deliveries trickle in. A breeze from the river beckons us. We find a little spot by the Brooklyn waterfront and spread out a soft fabric, enjoying the calm that hovers as the sun rises over the skyline. These moments are dear, and we take time to linger before the business of the day begins.

MENU

AVOCADO SANDWICHES WITH GREENS
AND PARSLEY PESTO

CONCENTRATED COFFEE AND MILK

DOUGHNUTS FROM YOUR LOCAL SHOP
(OR FOR OUR HOMEMADE RICOTTA FRITTERS
RECIPE, SEE PAGE 146)

MACERATED BLACKBERRIES
WITH BROWN SUGAR AND MINT

For a sunrise breakfast, bring strong concentrated
coffee, brewed and packed in a bottle the night before, to
accompany a quick sandwich made of hard-boiled eggs
and greens from the refrigerator. For sweets: some seasoned
berries and doughnuts from a local bakery.

Brooklyn, New York

AVOCADO SANDWICHES WITH GREENS AND PARSLEY PESTO

SERVES 2

Bright and summery, this sandwich has a nice clean bite—and for convenience, most of the components can be prepared the night before. In the morning, simply assemble and wrap in parchment paper.

---

1 cup packed fresh Italian parsley leaves

Pinch of coarse salt

⅓ cup olive oil

Place the parsley and coarse salt in a food processor and pulse until smooth. With the motor running, gradually pour in the olive oil, blending until the oil is fully incorporated. Adjust the seasoning if necessary.

2 eggs

1 teaspoon salt

2 brioche rolls, split

½ avocado, sliced

¼ teaspoon ground cumin

Juice of ½ lemon

½ cup fresh watercress or other fresh greens like baby lettuce or arugula

Put the eggs in a small pot, cover with cold water, and add the salt. Bring the water to a boil, remove the pot from the heat, cover it, and let it sit for 10 minutes. Drain the eggs, let them cool slightly, and then peel and slice into rounds.

Assemble the sandwiches by spreading the parsley pesto over the bottom of each brioche roll, then adding a layer of egg slices, followed by avocado slices, a sprinkle of cumin, a squeeze of lemon juice, and the greens. Cover with the tops of the brioche rolls.

CONCENTRATED COFFEE

MAKES 7 CUPS CONCENTRATED COFFEE

A batch of concentrated coffee will last for a month in your refrigerator, relieving you of one routine morning task. If you find this recipe daunting, you might just purchase a bottle. On cheat days we buy our favorite brand, Kickstand coffee concentrate, at our local shop.

½ pound ground coffee with chicory, or ½ pound dark-roast ground coffee

7 cups cold water

Half and half to taste

Honey to taste

In a large pitcher, stir together the coffee and cold water until all the ground coffee is wet; let stand at room temperature for 12 hours.

Pour the coffee mixture into another pitcher through a large fine-mesh strainer; discard the grounds. Clean the strainer; place a coffee filter or double layer of cheesecloth in the strainer, and pour the coffee mixture through the lined strainer into a clean pitcher. Cover and chill.

Use the concentrate to make iced coffee: In a tall glass, stir together ¼ cup of coffee concentrate and fill the glass with ice cubes and cold water. Add half and half and honey to your liking.

MACERATED BLACKBERRIES WITH BROWN SUGAR AND MINT

MAKES 2 CUPS

A sweet marinade is a great thing to do with your summer berries or stone fruit, and the longer they macerate the better. For dessert you can add whipped cream or ice cream. For breakfast, we keep this light and serve them over Greek yogurt or toast, or simply eat them alone for a sweet bite.

2 cups fresh blackberries

1 tablespoon coarse brown sugar

1 tablespoon agave nectar

¼ cup fresh mint leaves, torn

Combine the blackberries, brown sugar, agave, and mint leaves in a jar. Cover, and allow the berries to marinate overnight.

WINTER
BRUNCH

ON A COLD WINTER DAY we stay inside and make this lavish midmorning feast. The tea we brew warms us; we opt for a simple green tea from a favorite source, Bellocq tea shop in Greenpoint, Brooklyn. The addition of handmade details, such as a copper strainer and tea accessories handcrafted in Japan, elevates any brunch above the ordinary. To set the table, we keep a dark palette to complement the wintry bluster outside, using a beautiful piece of black linen as a tablecloth. A bowl or two filled with citrus fruit works as a centerpiece and offers a small jolt of color.

MENU

HOMEMADE EVERYTHING BAGELS

WHIPPED CREAM CHEESE

TEA AND GINGER-CURED SEA BASS

WARM CITRUS SALAD

FIG TART WITH HONEY

This tea brunch reminds me of Sunday mornings as a child, when
my father would pick up bagels, cream cheese, and smoked fish to
go with a lovely array of salads and cheeses assembled by my mother.
These Everything Bagels are adorned with black sesame seeds,
chia seeds, and rock salt and are served with whipped cream cheese
and house-cured sea bass. This meal is warm and nurturing, just
the thing for a cold winter day at home.

Brooklyn, New York

HOMEMADE EVERYTHING BAGELS

MAKES 12 SMALL BAGELS

We opted to top our bagels with coarse salt, sesame seeds, and chia seeds. If you don't have these handy, you can of course use any toppings of your choice: hemp seeds, poppy seeds, and dehydrated onion all work well.

3½ cups bread flour, plus extra for dusting

2 teaspoons sugar

2¼ teaspoons active dry yeast

2 teaspoons kosher salt

1⅓ cups warm water (about 105°F)

Vegetable oil, for the bowl

1 egg yolk

1 teaspoon water

1 tablespoon black sesame seeds

1 teaspoon chia seeds

1 teaspoon rock salt or coarse sea salt

In the bowl of a stand mixer fitted with the dough hook, combine the flour, sugar, yeast, and kosher salt. With the mixer on low speed, slowly add the warm water. Continue to mix until the dough comes together, 4 to 6 minutes.

Increase the speed to medium-high and knead for 8 to 10 minutes, until the dough is soft and smooth. Oil a large bowl, add the dough, and cover with a towel. Let the dough rise in a warm place until doubled in size, about 1 hour.

Gently punch down the dough and let rest for 10 minutes.

Preheat the oven to 425°F. Line a baking sheet with parchment paper. Bring a large pot of water to a boil, and then reduce to a simmer.

Divide the dough into 12 pieces. Press each piece to get rid of any air bubbles. Form them into smooth balls by rolling and rotating each one between your palms. Coat a finger with flour and press it through each ball to form a ring, stretching the dough and widening the hole to about one-third of the bagel's diameter. Place the bagels on the prepared baking sheet and cover with a towel. Let rest for 10 minutes. (If the bagels begin to dry out, spray them with a bit of water.)

Bring the water back to a full boil and gently lower the bagels, 2 or 3 at a time, into the water. Boil uncovered for about 1 minute. Flip and boil for another minute. Remove the bagels, drain, and return to the baking sheet.

Whisk the egg yolk with the 1 teaspoon water to create an egg wash. Using a pastry brush, coat the tops of the bagels with the egg wash. Sprinkle with the sesame seeds, chia seeds, and rock salt. Bake for 15 minutes or until golden. Transfer to a wire rack to cool completely.

WHIPPED CREAM CHEESE

MAKES ABOUT 2 CUPS

This great spread is simply upgraded cream cheese (a little lighter and a bit tart). You may choose to add chopped herbs like dill or basil to the mix—or even saffron would give it a nice touch.

One 8-ounce package cream cheese

2 tablespoons crème fraîche

¼ cup olive oil

Pinch of salt

In the bowl of a stand mixer fitted with the paddle attachment, combine the cream cheese, crème fraîche, olive oil, and salt. Whip on medium speed for about 2 minutes, until light and fluffy.

TEA AND GINGER–CURED SEA BASS

SERVES 4 TO 6

Curing fish is not as daunting as it sounds. Traditional recipes call for salmon and a standard salt mixture. We chose to play around a bit with less traditional flavors and found that tea leaves and ginger provide a very subtle but unique smokiness.

½ cup loose black tea leaves

½ cup rock salt

½ cup sugar

¼ cup black peppercorns

2 tablespoons water

3-inch nub fresh ginger, grated

One 1½-pound sea bass fillet, skin on, cut in half lengthwise to create 2 even fillets

Place the tea leaves, rock salt, sugar, peppercorns, and water in a bowl, and mix to combine.

Rub the grated ginger over the fish fillets.

Place two long pieces of plastic wrap in a "+" formation on a baking sheet. Place a layer of the curing mixture in the middle of the "+." Place one piece of fish, skin side down, on the curing mixture. Spread the remaining mixture evenly over the fish, and place the other fillet, skin side up, on top, creating a sandwich. Wrap the fish tightly in the plastic wrap. Place the wrapped fish on a metal rack set on top of a baking sheet. Set a heavy weight on the fish (a brick or some heavy canned goods will do). Refrigerate for 3 to 4 days.

Remove the fish from the plastic wrap and wipe off the remaining tea mixture with an absorbent towel. Remove the skin from the fillets, and using a thin, sharp knife, thinly slice the fish. Serve.

COOK'S NOTE | *The curing will take 3 to 4 days in the refrigerator, and the fish will keep for a few days after the curing mixture is removed. The longer you cure the fish, the saltier and more pronounced the flavors will become. Experiment to find what suits your taste.*

WARM CITRUS SALAD

SERVES 4 TO 6

I am always surprised at the beautiful citrus that winter offers us; perhaps it is nature's way of supplying us with much-needed vitamin C in those cold months. This layered salad works well with any variety of citrus fruits you might find at the market.

3 blood oranges

1 lemon

½ cup dry white wine

½ cup sugar

2 teaspoons honey

2 teaspoons chopped fresh rosemary

1 large pink grapefruit

3 clementines

Grate the zest of 1 blood orange. Juice the orange, and combine the juice and zest in a saucepan. Do the same with the lemon. Add the wine, sugar, honey, and rosemary. Bring to a boil, whisking to dissolve the sugar. Lower the heat and simmer until slightly thickened, about 15 minutes. Remove from the heat and let cool slightly.

Peel the remaining 2 blood oranges, the grapefruit, and the clementines, and slice into ¾-inch-thick rounds. Arrange the citrus rounds on a platter and pour the warm liquid over them. Serve warm.

COOK'S NOTE | *To peel citrus, cut off the top and bottom of the fruit, creating a flat surface on which to balance it. Place the edge of a sharp knife just inside the border where the pith meets the pulp, and slice down with a firm, clean stroke, following the curve of the fruit. Repeat until the entire fruit has been peeled.*

FIG TART WITH HONEY

SERVES 6

This tart is quite lovely, and it is one that you can prepare in advance. To do so, prebake your tart shell and mix the filling earlier in the day; store your filling in the refrigerator, then assemble the tart just before serving. You will likely have some of these ingredients on hand from the rest of the meal preparations for this menu. The filling is one of my favorites and has a perfect balance of sweet and tart. You can top this tart with any fruit that is in season—plums, persimmons, or berries would be lovely.

tart crust
2 cups all-purpose flour, plus extra for dusting

Pinch of salt

¼ cup sugar

1 cup (2 sticks) cold unsalted butter, cut into small cubes

½ cup ice water

filling
1 cup crème fraîche

1 cup cream cheese, softened

2 tablespoons sugar

Grated zest of 2 lemons

Juice of 1 lemon

15 to 20 fresh figs, sliced

Honey, for serving

Prepare the tart crust: In a food processor or by hand, combine the flour, salt, and sugar. Add the chilled butter cubes and process until the mixture resembles a coarse meal. Do not overmix; you want to retain some chunks of butter in order for the baked crust to be nice and flaky. Gradually add the ice water until the dough just comes together. Form the dough into a ball, wrap it in plastic wrap, and chill it in the refrigerator for 20 minutes.

Lightly flour your work surface (preferably a cold surface), and roll out the dough to form a ¼-inch-thick rectangle, about 5 × 14 inches. (If the dough cracks while you're rolling it, just pinch it back together.) Fit the dough into a 4½ × 13¾-inch tart pan (preferably nonstick). Cut off any excess dough. Prick the bottom of the dough with a fork to prevent it from rising. Refrigerate the tart shell for 15 minutes.

Meanwhile, preheat the oven to 350°F.

Place parchment paper on top of the chilled tart shell and fill it with pie weights or dried beans. Bake for 20 to 25 minutes, until golden. Allow the crust to cool completely.

Make the filling: In a bowl, stir together the crème fraîche, cream cheese, sugar, lemon zest, and lemon juice.

Fill the cooled tart shell with the cream filling, and arrange the figs in rows on top. Serve immediately, drizzled with honey.

NOON

CAMPING

WE BRING BLANKETS AND INVITE FRIENDS to sit fireside amid the trees and the foliage. While some build the fire, others gather branches and leaves to take home as tokens. We enjoy a meal of warm shakshuka, naan, hummus, and a few other accompaniments. The damp, cool air of the Pacific coast feels refreshing and sweet, as does the crunch of the leaves beneath our boots.

MENU

SHAKSHUKA

LEMON HUMMUS

NAAN WITH ROSEMARY AND THYME

CHARRED ASPARAGUS

BRAISED RAPINI

CINNAMON-SUGAR POPCORN

FIELD GUIDE

BLANKETS

FIREWOOD

TEAKETTLE

POCKETKNIFE

CAN OPENER

CAST-IRON SKILLETS

ALUMINUM FOIL

CONTAINERS FOR LEFTOVERS

This camper's lunch is fit for a crisp, cool day, though one doesn't have
to travel far to cook outdoors. We built a fire near our friend's cabin in
Oregon. While we were close enough to a kitchen to walk a few items over,
this meal can be made entirely campside if preferred.

Williams Residence
Portland, Oregon

SHAKSHUKA

SERVES 4 TO 6

A gorgeous stew of tomatoes, peppers, and herbs feels like home on a plate. Historically we have made this for a late breakfast and sometimes for dinner. Served with lots of bread for dipping, every morsel is usually devoured. Many have expanded on this tradition and added greens, cheeses, and other vegetables to the dish—this version is in its traditional form. The most important thing is to be sure to use great-quality eggs, farm-fresh if possible—you will thank us.

3 tablespoons olive oil, plus more for drizzling

1 green bell or other bell pepper, chopped into 1-inch pieces

1 bay leaf

1 medium onion, diced

3 cloves garlic, thinly sliced

2 teaspoons harissa
(see Cook's Note)

½ teaspoon salt, plus extra for seasoning

1 teaspoon freshly ground black pepper, plus extra for seasoning

1 teaspoon smoked paprika

¼ teaspoon fennel seeds, crushed

¾ teaspoon ground cumin

½ teaspoon ground coriander

1 pound ripe tomatoes, cored and diced

One 14-ounce can diced or crushed tomatoes (San Marzano work nicely)

2 tablespoons tomato paste

6 eggs

½ cup chopped fresh parsley leaves

In a wide skillet, heat the olive oil over medium-high heat. Add the pepper, bay leaf, onion, and garlic and cook for 5 minutes, until the onion is soft and wilted. Add the harissa, salt, pepper, paprika, fennel, cumin, and coriander. Cook for a minute, stirring constantly, to release the fragrance.

Add the ripe and canned tomatoes and the tomato paste, and reduce the heat to medium. Cook for 12 to 15 minutes, until the sauce has thickened.

With the back of a spoon, make six indentations in the sauce. Crack an egg into each indentation. Season the eggs with salt and pepper, and drizzle with olive oil. Cover, reduce the heat to a simmer, and cook until the eggs are done to your liking, 10 to 15 minutes. Garnish with the parsley, and serve.

COOK'S NOTE | *Harissa, a Tunisian hot sauce, incorporates a variety of peppers—piri piri, serrano—with lemon juice and herbs and spices such as garlic, cumin, and coriander. You can purchase harissa at specialty stores or online grocers.*

LEMON HUMMUS

SERVES 6 TO 8

Fluffy and creamy with a nice tart hit of preserved lemon, this hummus can be made a few days in advance and will keep in an airtight jar for about a week. At the meal, serve it topped with a flaky salt and grated lemon zest, and of course alongside a great bread like our Naan with Rosemary and Thyme.

---

2 cups dried chickpeas

6 cups water

2 tablespoons tahini

2 teaspoons salt

Freshly ground black pepper

1 clove garlic

1 preserved lemon

Grated zest and juice of 1 lemon

2 tablespoons olive oil

1 cup plus 1 tablespoon ice water

Maldon sea salt for garnish

Place the chickpeas in a large bowl, cover with cold water by 2 inches, and soak for 8 hours or overnight.

Drain the chickpeas, and combine them with the 6 cups water in a large saucepan. Bring to a boil, reduce the heat, and simmer for about 1½ hours, until the chickpeas shed their skins but are not overly soft. Drain, discarding the skins that have fallen off.

Place the chickpeas, tahini, salt, pepper, garlic, preserved lemon, and lemon juice in a blender or food processor. Blend on medium speed, gradually adding the olive oil, followed by the ice water until the hummus has the consistency you prefer.

Serve topped with the grated lemon zest and sea salt.

NAAN WITH ROSEMARY AND THYME

MAKES 12 PIECES

The trick to this bread is a bit of kitchen confidence; it truly is not as tough as it sounds. The beautiful char can be made over the fire or over a stove's flame in your own kitchen. We highly recommend serving it with lots of herbs and ghee.

1½ teaspoons sugar

½ cup warm water (about 105°F)

2½ teaspoons active dry yeast

4 cups all-purpose flour,
plus extra for dusting

1½ teaspoons salt

¼ teaspoon baking soda

5 tablespoons olive oil, plus extra
for the bowl and the skillet

1 cup plain yogurt

1 teaspoon chopped fresh rosemary
leaves

1 teaspoon chopped fresh
thyme leaves

Ghee (recipe follows) or unsalted
butter, melted, for serving

In a small bowl, dissolve the sugar in the warm water. Add the yeast and stir until it has dissolved. Cover and set aside for 10 minutes or until bubbles form.

Flour a flat surface like a large cutting board or a kitchen counter.

In a large mixing bowl, sift the flour, salt, and baking soda together. Add the olive oil, yogurt, and yeast mixture to the flour. Use your fingers to mix all the ingredients together until you can pull the mixture into a soft dough. It should be soft but not sticky. Knead the dough on the floured surface for about 5 minutes, until it is soft and stretchy.

Place the dough in a lightly oiled bowl, brush the surface of the dough with some oil, cover with a towel, and set it aside in a warm place until it has doubled in size, about 2 hours.

Punch the dough down, knead it again for about 4 minutes, and then shape it into a ball. Divide the dough into 12 equal portions, place on a floured surface in a warm place, cover, and allow to rise for another 30 to 45 minutes.

Roll out each portion of dough on a lightly floured surface to create an elongated oval about ⅛ inch thick. Sprinkle the tops of the ovals with the rosemary and thyme.

Heat a nonstick or cast-iron skillet over very high heat, and generously coat the bottom of the skillet with olive oil. Place the dough in the skillet, one at a time, cover it quickly, reduce the heat to medium, and allow the bread to bubble for 1 to 2 minutes.

Using tongs, remove the bread from the skillet and cook the other side of each piece over the direct flame of a gas burner. The naan usually puffs up, and some spots will get charred (which imparts the lovely smoky flavor).

Remove from the heat and brush generously with melted ghee or butter. Repeat with the remaining dough.

GHEE

MAKES ½ CUP

Found to be highly beneficial in Ayurvedic medicine as well as many Eastern diets, ghee is a form of clarified butter that is used for sautés and as a spread. Once made and sealed in an airtight container, it has a long shelf life.

8 tablespoons (1 stick) unsalted butter

Heat the butter in a saucepan over low heat for about an hour. Strain the clarified butter through a fine-mesh strainer into a container, and discard the solids in the strainer. Store at room temperature for up to 1 month.

CHARRED ASPARAGUS

SERVES 4 TO 6

High heat leaves these asparagus perfectly cooked with a bit of a smoky char that is comforting and campside-appropriate.

2 bunches fresh asparagus

¼ cup olive oil

Sea salt and freshly ground black pepper to taste

4 cloves garlic, smashed

1 lemon, sliced

Preheat the oven to 450°F. Line a baking sheet with parchment paper.

Spread the asparagus out on the prepared baking sheet, and sprinkle with the olive oil. Season with sea salt and pepper, and toss to coat. Add the smashed garlic and top with the lemon slices. Roast for 15 to 20 minutes, until lightly charred.

COOK'S NOTE | *If you are preparing this on the campfire, coat the asparagus with the olive oil and season with sea salt and pepper. Then cook the spears directly on the grill over a high flame for about 5 minutes, being sure to flip them over about halfway through.*

BRAISED RAPINI

SERVES 4 TO 6

We found a beautiful purple rapini at the market and simply couldn't resist; however, you could substitute any greens here. This sauté is a classic and works well indoors and out.

2 tablespoons olive oil

1 clove garlic, smashed

1 large bunch rapini
(or other greens like kale
or mustard greens)

Salt and freshly ground black pepper to taste

Heat a medium skillet over high heat. Add the oil and garlic, and sauté for 1 to 2 minutes, until fragrant. Add the rapini, season with salt and pepper, reduce the heat to medium-high, and cook for 3 to 5 minutes, until slightly tender. Remove the garlic clove, and serve.

CINNAMON-SUGAR POPCORN

MAKES 8 CUPS

This dessert caused quite a stir with our friends. The simple combination of cinnamon and sugar as an unexpected topping was marvelous; we even added a pinch of salt for a savory touch.

1½ teaspoons ground cinnamon

¼ cup sugar

3 tablespoons coconut, peanut, or grapeseed oil (or other oil with a high smoke point)

⅓ cup good-quality popcorn kernels

3 tablespoons unsalted butter, melted

Fine sea salt to taste

Combine the cinnamon and sugar in a small bowl, and set aside.

Heat the coconut oil in a 3-quart saucepan over medium-high heat. Add 3 or 4 popcorn kernels to the oil and cover the pan.

When the kernels pop, add the rest of the popcorn kernels in an even layer. Cover the pan, remove from the heat, and let sit for 30 seconds. Once the kernels begin popping, return the pan to the burner and cook, gently shaking the pan back and forth. Try to keep the lid slightly ajar to let the steam release (so the popcorn will be drier and crisper). Once the popping slows to several seconds between pops, remove the pan from the heat and dump the popcorn into a wide bowl. Add the melted butter and the cinnamon sugar, tossing to coat evenly. Sprinkle with sea salt, and serve.

DAY TRIP

WHEN WEATHER PERMITS, we leave the city for a dose of nature. We venture to orchards, farms, zoos, and parks. A picnic basket overflowing with sandwiches and homemade snacks keeps us satiated on a long journey. We play road-trip tunes and marvel at the open spaces ahead.

MENU

FRIED GREEN TOMATO SANDWICHES WITH
MINT MAYO AND WATERCRESS

WATERMELON SALAD WITH LEMON AND
CORIANDER SEED DRESSING

BRIOCHE ROLLS

HOMEMADE HAZELNUT SPREAD

PICKLED GRAPES

———————

This menu is a better-than-average picnic: fried green tomato
sandwiches, pickled fruits, watermelon salad, and brioche
with homemade hazelnut spread. Be sure to throw in some
extra nibbles like cured meats, olives, and cheeses.

FRIED GREEN TOMATO SANDWICHES WITH MINT MAYO AND WATERCRESS

MAKES 6 SANDWICHES

At summer's end you will likely find beautiful green tomatoes in great bounty at the farmers' market. They are firm and tart and work well in jams, pickles, and chutneys. We love them best fried, slathered with green mayo, and sandwiched between slices of freshly baked bread.

---

sandwiches

3 to 4 green tomatoes, sliced ½ inch thick (12 slices total)

Salt and freshly ground black pepper

1 cup all-purpose flour

3 eggs

2 tablespoons whole milk

1 cup yellow cornmeal

1 cup dried breadcrumbs

¼ teaspoon chili powder

1 cup canola oil

1 teaspoon kosher salt

12 slices whole-grain bread, toasted

2 cups fresh watercress or arugula

mint mayo

2 egg yolks

Juice of ½ lemon, plus extra for seasoning

¼ teaspoon salt, plus extra for seasoning

½ cup fresh mint leaves

1 cup canola or safflower oil

Line a baking sheet with paper towels. Line up the tomato slices on a separate baking sheet, and salt and pepper both sides.

Set up a three-bowl breading station: Your first bowl should contain the flour, the second a well-blended mixture of the eggs and milk, and the third the cornmeal and breadcrumbs whisked together. Season each bowl with ½ teaspoon salt, a pinch of black pepper, and a pinch of chili powder.

Bread both sides of the tomato slices in the flour, then dip each slice into the egg-milk mixture, and finally coat the slices with the cornmeal mixture, making sure that each piece is thickly coated.

Heat the oil in a cast-iron or other heavy skillet over medium-high heat. In batches, fry the tomatoes for 3 to 5 minutes on each side, until golden. Transfer the slices to the paper-towel-lined baking sheet to drain. Sprinkle with the kosher salt. Carefully wipe the skillet clean with paper towels after frying each batch.

Make the mint mayo: In a food processor, combine the egg yolks, lemon juice, and salt; process for 30 seconds. Add the mint and process for a more few seconds, until just combined.

With the motor running, add the oil in a slow stream. If the mayo becomes too thick, thin it with water. Season the mayo with more salt and/or lemon juice to taste.

Slather each piece of bread with 1 tablespoon of Mint Mayo; refrigerate the remaining mayo. Top 6 slices of toast with 2 fried green tomatoes each, add a handful of watercress or arugula, and top with the remaining slices of toast.

WATERMELON SALAD WITH LEMON AND CORIANDER SEED DRESSING

SERVES 6

This bright salad features a great mix of fruits and vegetables and teaches us to explore possibilities beyond the leafy greens in the market.

---

1 Asian pear, cubed

Juice of ½ lemon

dressing
½ teaspoon coriander seeds

Juice of 2 lemons

3 tablespoons sugar

½ teaspoon salt

¼ teaspoon freshly cracked black pepper

¼ cup olive oil

3 cups cubed watermelon

1 cup cherry tomatoes, halved

1 cup cubed mixed radishes and turnips

2 tablespoons finely chopped fresh parsley

2 tablespoons finely chopped fresh basil

5 cups mixed salad greens

Combine the pear cubes with the lemon juice in a small bowl, and set aside.

Make the dressing: Toast the coriander seeds in a skillet set over medium heat until light golden. Then grind the seeds fine with a mortar and pestle. Combine the ground coriander, lemon juice, sugar, salt, and pepper in a bowl and whisk to dissolve the sugar. Slowly whisk in the oil.

Drain the pear and place the cubes in a salad bowl. Add the watermelon, cherry tomatoes, radishes and turnips, parsley, and basil. Toss to combine. Add the salad greens, toss again, and drizzle with the dressing. Serve immediately.

BRIOCHE ROLLS

MAKES 16 SMALL ROLLS

These soft rolls, known in France as *brioche à tête,* are traditionally baked in small flared metal tins. The bread is puffy and buttery and the *tête* quite literally is a small head atop the larger bun.

½ cup whole milk, warmed (about 110°F)

1 tablespoon active dry yeast

2¼ cups all-purpose flour, plus extra for dusting

3 tablespoons sugar

½ teaspoon salt

3 large eggs

8 tablespoons (1 stick) unsalted butter, cut into 1-tablespoon pieces

Vegetable oil

1 tablespoon heavy cream

Combine the warm milk, yeast, and 1 cup of the flour in a small bowl and let sit for 5 minutes, until bubbles form.

In the bowl of a stand mixer fitted with the paddle attachment, mix the remaining 1¼ cups flour, sugar, and salt.

In a separate bowl, whisk 2 of the eggs. Add the eggs and the yeast mixture to the flour and mix on medium speed, dropping the butter pieces in one at a time.

Remove the paddle and fit the mixer with the dough hook. Knead the mixture for 10 minutes on medium-high speed, until the dough is smooth and elastic. Transfer the dough to an oiled bowl, cover with plastic wrap, and allow to rest in a warm spot for 1 to 2 hours, until doubled in size.

Place the dough on a generously floured surface and mold it into a ball. Divide the ball into 16 pieces. Shape each portion into a ball by cupping your hand around the dough and gently rolling it. Take each ball and carefully pinch a bit together to create a smaller ball on top, which is still attached by a "stem" of dough.

Grease 16 brioche tins or 16 cups of two standard muffin tins. Transfer the dough balls to the brioche tins, with the tête on top.

Cover the tins with a towel and allow the dough to rise in a warm spot for 1 hour.

Preheat the oven to 350°F.

In a small bowl, whisk the remaining egg with the heavy cream. Lightly brush the tops of the brioche rolls with this glaze. Bake for about 20 minutes, until golden brown. Allow the rolls to cool in their tins for 5 minutes, and then transfer to a wire rack to cool completely.

HOMEMADE HAZELNUT SPREAD

MAKES 1 CUP

This homemade version of Nutella can be made completely from scratch or with fresh-ground hazelnut butter. A Vitamix is recommended for the best results, but a standard blender along with some determination will do. Either way, you may never go back to the store-bought form.

2 cups hazelnuts, roasted and peeled

¼ cup sweetened dark chocolate, melted

Pinch of salt

Process the hazelnuts in a food processor for 10 minutes until finely ground. Transfer to a blender, and blend for 3 minutes. If the nut butter is too thick, add water, 1 tablespoon at time, to reach the desired consistency.

In a medium bowl, mix the hazelnut butter with the melted chocolate and season with salt to taste. The spread will keep for 1 week in the refrigerator. Be sure to bring it to room temperature before serving.

PICKLED GRAPES

MAKES ABOUT 3 CUPS

Offbeat pickles are always a fun undertaking, especially at summer's end. These fruit pickles offer that extra dimension of flavor to fill out a salad, sandwich, or cheese plate.

1 pound red or black grapes, preferably seedless

1 cup white wine vinegar

1 cup sugar

1 bay leaf

1 teaspoon black peppercorns

1 whole clove

Pinch of salt

Remove the grapes from the stems and place them in a heat-proof bowl.

Combine the vinegar, sugar, bay leaf, peppercorns, clove, and salt in a saucepan and cook over low heat until the sugar has dissolved. Pour over the grapes. Remove the cloves and peppercorns. Cover and refrigerate for 8 hours or overnight.

A PACKED MEAL

LEAVING OUR CITY MUSINGS BEHIND, we drive out in search of trees and expanse. Among the redwoods of San Francisco we spread out a worn canvas and arrange a feast of extravagant picnic fare. The scenery is spectacular, and the air feels cleaner and fresher than one can imagine. The filling meal allows us to stay longer and enjoy a day in the forest. Of course, not everyone has access to beautiful redwoods, but do seek out your own patch of woods and take a moment. It will surely be worth the preparations.

MENU

BEET PICKLED EGGS

BUTTERMILK FRIED CHICKEN

POTATO TART WITH BLACK OLIVES

CHOPPED KALE SALAD WITH
GREEN DRESSING AND CREMA

MULLED WINE

APPLE CIDER CAKES

FRESH FRUIT

This feast is meant to please a crowd with favorites like fried chicken
and chopped salad, along with a few less expected items like beet pickled
eggs and mulled wine. Be sure to stop at the market or a roadside stand on
your way for some fresh fruit as well; we found a sweet watermelon
en route and added it to the meal.

Redwood Forest, California

BEET PICKLED EGGS

SERVES 6 TO 10

These hard-boiled eggs have a hit of color and tartness and would also make a spunky deviled egg for a party.

3 cups water

1 cup distilled white vinegar

1 small beet, sliced

1 small shallot, sliced

1 teaspoon sugar

½ teaspoon salt

1 bay leaf

12 hard-boiled large eggs, peeled

Flaky salt, such as Maldon, for serving

Combine the water, vinegar, beet, shallot, sugar, salt, and bay leaf in a 2-quart saucepan and bring to a boil. Reduce the heat, cover the pan, and simmer until the beet slices are tender, about 20 minutes. Uncover and let cool completely.

Place the beet mixture in a container, add the eggs, and marinate in the refrigerator for at least 2 hours, stirring gently once or twice.

To serve, slice the eggs in half and top with flaky salt.

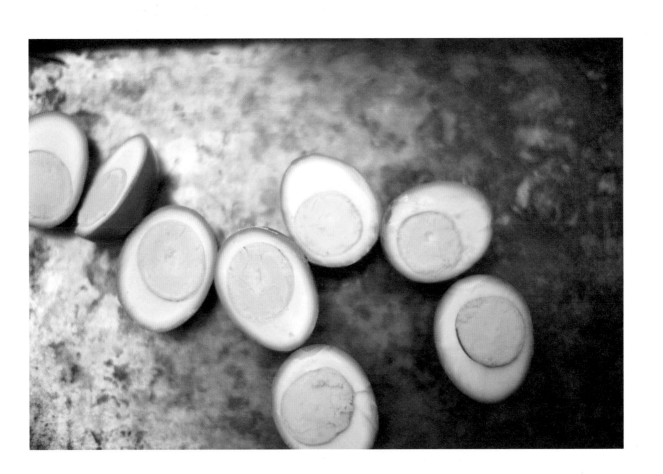

BUTTERMILK FRIED CHICKEN

SERVES 6

An overnight brine imparts all the flavor and moistness of a good fried chicken. The coating is dark, tasty, and perfectly flaky. We like to throw a bit of flaky salt atop before serving.

---

6 chicken drumsticks

6 chicken thighs

4 quarts vegetable oil

Flaky salt, such as Maldon

brine
1 tablespoon olive oil

1 large red onion, cut into wedges

1 poblano chile, seeded
and cut into 1-inch pieces

5 cloves garlic, cut in half

1 teaspoon black
peppercorns, crushed

10 sprigs fresh thyme

2 sprigs fresh rosemary

4 bay leaves

Zest of 1 lemon, removed in strips

Juice of 1 lemon

4 cups buttermilk

2 tablespoons kosher salt

breading
2½ cups all-purpose flour

3 tablespoons coarsely ground
black pepper

2 tablespoons smoked paprika

1 tablespoon kosher salt

½ teaspoon cayenne pepper

1 teaspoon chili powder

2 tablespoons baking powder

2 cups buttermilk

Rinse the chicken pieces and pat dry. Using a small paring knife, score the chicken along the bones to ensure that it cooks though.

Prepare the brine: Heat the olive oil in a large skillet over medium heat. Add the onion, poblano chile, and garlic, and cook for 3 to 5 minutes, until the onion is soft. Add the peppercorns, thyme sprigs, rosemary sprigs, and bay leaves, and cook until the aromatics are fragrant, about 2 minutes.

Put the lemon zest and juice in a large bowl. Add the buttermilk and kosher salt, and stir in the onion mixture.

Place the chicken and the brine in a large brining bag or other sturdy plastic bag. (You may want to place the bag in a bowl for support.) Remove as much air as possible when sealing the bag, and be sure that the chicken is completely covered with brining liquid. Allow the chicken to marinate for 8 hours or overnight in the refrigerator.

Remove the chicken from the bag, and rinse and pat dry. Allow it to air-dry further while you set up the breading station: In a medium-size bowl, combine the flour with the black pepper, paprika, kosher salt, cayenne, chili powder, and baking powder. Fill another bowl with the buttermilk.

Dip each piece of chicken into the flour mixture, then into the buttermilk, and then back into the flour.

Attach a deep-frying thermometer to a deep saucepan or Dutch oven, add the vegetable oil, and heat it to 350°F. Fry the chicken for 12 to 15 minutes, until golden brown. Remove the chicken from the oil and allow it to rest on a cooling rack for 10 minutes.

Sprinkle with a flaky salt before serving.

POTATO TART WITH BLACK OLIVES

SERVES 6 TO 8

This tart is something between a Spanish tortilla and a savory galette. It is a nice way to rethink the potato, and by omitting a crust it feels light enough to balance the rest of the meal.

2½ pounds (5 to 6 large) Yukon Gold potatoes, sliced ⅛ inch thick

1 tablespoon unsalted butter

½ cup black olives, chopped

1 red onion, sliced

3 cloves garlic, minced

½ teaspoon chopped fresh rosemary

4 tablespoons (½ stick) unsalted butter, melted

1 tablespoon cornstarch

1 teaspoon salt

½ teaspoon freshly ground black pepper

Nonstick cooking spray

Preheat the oven to 450°F.

Place the potatoes in a large bowl and add cold water to cover. Stir to remove the excess starch, then drain. Spread the slices out on kitchen towels and dry thoroughly.

Melt the 1 tablespoon butter in a skillet over medium heat. Add the olives, onion, garlic, and rosemary and cook for 3 to 5 minutes, until the onions are soft. Set aside.

In a large bowl, whisk 3 tablespoons of the melted butter with the cornstarch, salt, and pepper. Add the dried potatoes and toss until they are thoroughly coated.

Brush the remaining 1 tablespoon melted butter over the bottom of a 10-inch ovenproof skillet. Place 1 potato slice in the center of the skillet, and then overlap slices in a circle around the center slice, using half of the slices. Sprinkle the olive mixture over the potatoes. Arrange the remaining potatoes on top to form an even layer.

Place the skillet over medium-high heat and cook until the potatoes have started to turn translucent around the edges, about 5 minutes. Spray a piece of aluminum foil with nonstick cooking spray. Place the foil, sprayed side down, on top of the potatoes. Place a 9-inch cake pan on top of the foil, and use a heavy weight, such as a brick or pie weights. Transfer the skillet to the oven and bake for 20 minutes.

Remove the cake pan and foil from the skillet. Bake until tender, 20 to 25 minutes.

Place the skillet over medium heat and cook, shaking it gently (use a potholder—the handle will be hot), until the tart releases from the sides of the skillet, 2 to 3 minutes. Remove the skillet from the heat and place a cutting board over the skillet. Carefully invert the skillet and cutting board together. Lift the skillet off the tart. Using a serrated knife, gently cut the tart into wedges and serve warm.

CHOPPED KALE SALAD WITH GREEN DRESSING AND CREMA

SERVES 4 TO 6

Kale salad is our go-to lunch at the studio—it is fast, healthful, and light. This dressing is a godsend; it might change your life. Try it on fish, salads, or drizzled into soups. We happened to have some Mexican crema in our fridge, which gave a final tartness to the salad. You can find crema at a local Mexican grocery, but a good-quality plain yogurt will also do the trick.

---

salad

½ pound rapini or other greens

2 cloves garlic, smashed

2 tablespoons olive oil

½ teaspoon salt

Freshly ground black pepper to taste

1 bunch Lacinato kale

1 bunch baby turnips

½ small savoy cabbage

1 scallion

dressing

½ cup fresh mint leaves

½ cup fresh cilantro leaves

1 cup fresh parsley leaves

¼ cup olive oil

1 tablespoon distilled white vinegar

1 teaspoon salt, plus more if needed

Juice of ¼ lemon

1 cup Mexican crema or plain yogurt

Preheat the oven to 400°F. Line a baking dish with parchment paper.

In a small bowl, toss the rapini, garlic, olive oil, and salt and pepper. Transfer the greens to the prepared baking dish and roast for 15 to 20 minutes, until slightly charred.

While the greens are roasting, chop the kale and turnips, shred the cabbage, and slice the scallion.

Make the dressing: Combine the mint, cilantro, parsley, oil, vinegar, salt, and lemon juice in a blender, and blend for 2 to 3 minutes. Taste, and season with more salt if desired.

Toss the chopped salad with the roasted rapini. Add the dressing, toss again, and top with a generous spoonful of crema.

MULLED WINE

SERVES 6

Warm and comforting, a well-seasoned mulled wine is a nice accompaniment for an outdoor trip with friends. As it heats on your stove, the spices will fill the room with a beautiful aroma. Pack this beverage in a thermos and bring it along for a taste of home.

4 cups apple cider

One 750-ml bottle red wine, such as Cabernet Sauvignon

¼ cup honey

2 cinnamon sticks

Zest and juice of 1 orange

4 whole cloves

3 whole star anise

Peel of 4 oranges, removed in strips with a vegetable peeler, for garnish

Combine the cider, wine, honey, cinnamon sticks, orange zest, orange juice, cloves, and star anise in a large saucepan. Bring to a boil, reduce the heat to low, and simmer for 10 minutes.

Strain the mulled wine into 6 mugs, add a strip of orange peel to each one, and serve.

APPLE CIDER CAKES

MAKES 17 MINI CAKES

Moist and perfectly sweet, these little cakes go well with a glass of mulled wine or a cup of rose tea on a cool day.

Nonstick spray or unsalted butter, for the pans

1½ cups all-purpose flour

½ teaspoon baking powder

1 teaspoon baking soda

½ teaspoon salt

½ teaspoon ground cinnamon

¼ teaspoon ground cardamom

¾ cup olive oil

¾ cup sugar

1 teaspoon vanilla extract

1½ cups apple cider

½ cup applesauce

topping

½ cup sugar

¼ teaspoon ground cinnamon

Preheat the oven to 375°F. Grease 12 cavities of a mini Bundt cake pan plus 5 additional cavities of a second pan with nonstick cooking spray or melted butter.

In a large mixing bowl, combine the flour, baking powder, baking soda, salt, cinnamon, and cardamom, and stir well.

In another large bowl, combine the olive oil, sugar, vanilla, cider, and applesauce, and mix well. Slowly add the wet ingredients to the dry, and incorporate well. Pour the batter into the greased molds, filling each mold three-quarters of the way (leaving room for the cakes to rise).

Make the topping: Combine the sugar and cinnamon in a small bowl, and set aside.

Bake the cakes for 15 minutes, until a toothpick inserted into the center of a cake comes out dry.

Allow the cakes to cool for 5 minutes in their pans. Then remove from the pans and immediately roll the top of the cakes in the cinnamon sugar.

SPRING
FORAGER'S
LUNCH

THE FIRST SIGNS OF SPRINGTIME in New York are highly antic-
ipated and warmly welcomed. The farmers' market is full of exciting new
prospects. With a hop in our step we gather ramps, fresh breads, and gorgeous
Araucana eggs from a local farm.

MENU

GREEN SOUP WITH LEMON-CUMIN YOGURT

MUSHROOM TOAST WITH SOFT-COOKED EGGS

ROASTED SPRING VEGETABLES

––––––––––––––

This meal comes together easily, and is a simple-man's lunch.
Serve it with great bread and rich butter.

GREEN SOUP WITH LEMON-CUMIN YOGURT

SERVES 6

Brightly colored, this beautiful soup is a nice way to get your greens in. The drizzle of yogurt adds a welcome complexity.

2 tablespoons olive oil

1 tablespoon unsalted butter

1 spring garlic, sliced

2 shallots, chopped

3 cloves garlic, chopped

2 bay leaves

4 cups organic chicken stock

6 cups chopped fresh spinach leaves

2 cups peas, fresh or frozen

½ cup chopped fresh watercress or mint

Salt and freshly ground black pepper to taste

Lemon-Cumin Yogurt (recipe follows)

Freshly cracked black pepper, for serving

Heat the oil and butter in a large saucepan over medium heat. Add the spring garlic, shallots, garlic, and bay leaves and sauté for a few minutes, until slightly browned. Add the stock and bring to a boil. Add the spinach, peas, and watercress or mint. Cook for a few minutes, just until the peas are cooked through but still bright green. Season with salt and pepper. Remove the pot from the heat and discard the bay leaves.

Carefully puree the soup with an immersion blender or in a standard blender (be cautious when blending hot liquids). Top with Lemon-Cumin Yogurt, sprinkle with pepper, and serve.

LEMON-CUMIN YOGURT

MAKES 1 CUP

1 cup whole-milk yogurt

1 teaspoon grated lemon zest

Juice of ½ lemon

1 tablespoon olive oil

¼ teaspoon ground cumin

Pinch of salt

In a small bowl, whisk the yogurt, lemon zest, lemon juice, olive oil, cumin, and salt together until well combined. Refrigerate, covered, until serving time. The yogurt will keep in the refrigerator for up to 3 days.

MUSHROOM TOAST WITH SOFT-COOKED EGGS

SERVES 4

Inspired by a recent foraging trip in the woods, this toast is a beautiful assembly of flavors. You can certainly experiment with the varieties of mushrooms available.

4 thick slices country bread

6 tablespoons extra virgin olive oil, plus extra for the bread

1 clove garlic, cut in half or smashed

1 tablespoon butter

6 cups assorted wild mushrooms, chopped

½ teaspoon sea salt

1 sprig fresh rosemary

Juice of ½ lemon

4 large organic eggs

Salt and freshly ground black pepper to taste

4 tablespoons crème fraîche

Preheat the oven to 450°F.

Brush the bread slices with olive oil and transfer them to a baking sheet. Toast the bread in the oven, flipping the slices over once, until golden brown, about 8 minutes. Rub the garlic clove over the toast.

Heat 2 tablespoons of the olive oil and the butter in a large cast-iron or nonstick skillet. Add the mushrooms, sea salt, and rosemary sprig, and sauté for about 5 minutes, until the mushrooms have softened. Remove from the heat and drizzle the lemon juice over the mushrooms. Remove the sprig of rosemary.

Meanwhile, heat the remaining 4 tablespoons oil in a large nonstick skillet over low heat. Crack each egg individually into a small bowl and then pour the egg into the skillet, being careful not to break the yolk. Cover and cook for a few minutes, until the whites have cooked but the yolks are still a bit runny. Season with salt and pepper.

To assemble the toast, spread 1 tablespoon of the crème fraîche over each slice, followed by about 2 tablespoons of the cooked mushrooms, and finally a fried egg. Enjoy.

ROASTED SPRING VEGETABLES

SERVES 6

Roasting vegetables may seem to be a wintry practice, but we enjoy it year-round. The crisp and sweet result is a favorite in our home, especially for weeknight suppers. Here we call on the season's early bounty, perfect for a chilly spring day.

---

2 parsnips, cut into 3-inch pieces

6 medium sunchokes, cut into 2-inch chunks

1 lemon: one half juiced, the other half sliced

1 sprig fresh rosemary

2 cloves garlic, smashed

¼ cup plus 1 tablespoon olive oil

2 bundles ramps

Salt to taste

Preheat the oven to 400°F.

In a large bowl, combine the parsnips, sunchokes, lemon juice and slices, rosemary sprig, and garlic cloves. Add the ¼ cup olive oil, and toss well. Transfer the mixture to a large baking dish and roast for 20 minutes.

Meanwhile, rinse and dry the ramps thoroughly. Toss the ramps with the remaining 1 tablespoon olive oil and a sprinkle of salt.

Add the ramps to the baking dish and roast for another 20 minutes.

COOK'S NOTE | *Ramps, or wild leeks, are an early spring vegetable, and are usually in season for a small window of time. They are a cross between garlic and onion in both taste and scent. Ramps work well sautéed, roasted, and pickled.*

AFTERNOON

CITY
PICNIC

IN A BUSTLING CITY THAT EXCITES US DAILY, we often seek out moments of respite. This waterfront picnic brings together friends and great food to create a small urban hideaway, tucked away from the busyness of our city living. The menu is playful; the friends are new and old. As the sun graciously sets over Manhattan, we enjoy our meal and go back for extra helpings.

MENU

NIGELLA CHICKEN PIES WITH BABY CARROTS

RICE, ZUCCHINI, AND FETA FRITTATA
WITH FENNEL POLLEN YOGURT

BURRATA SALAD WITH SPICY
CAULIFLOWER RELISH AND CROSTINI

FENNEL SLAW WITH PICKLED RED ONIONS,
RAISINS, HAZELNUTS, AND MINT

TOMATO AND CANTALOUPE SALAD

Pre-portion the Burrata salad into glass jars for transporting;
with individual meat pies and slices of frittata, this meal becomes
mostly finger-friendly. Put out some flavored sodas and bring
along some wildflowers for a bit of whimsy.

South Williamsburg, New York

NIGELLA CHICKEN PIES WITH BABY CARROTS

SERVES 8 TO 10

These individual pies combine the comfort and gratification of a traditional meat pie with the portability that is perfect for a picnic.

savory pie dough

3¾ cups all-purpose flour, plus extra for dusting

1 tablespoon sugar

1¾ teaspoons salt

20 twists of a pepper mill

12 tablespoons (1½ sticks) cold unsalted butter, cut into cubes

1¼ cups ice-cold water

Make the pie dough: Combine the flour, sugar, salt, and pepper in a food processor and mix well. Add the butter and pulse until the mixture forms pea-size pieces. Working with ¼ cup of the ice water at a time, add water while pulsing the processor, stopping once the dough starts to come together. Set the dough on a piece of plastic wrap, flatten it into a thick disk, and wrap. Allow the dough to rest in the refrigerator for at least 30 minutes. (The dough will keep in your refrigerator for up to 1 week or in the freezer for a few months.)

Make the pie filling: In a large sauté pan, gently warm the olive oil over low heat. Add the chiles and cook for 2 minutes. Increase the heat to medium-high, add the onion, and sauté until soft, about 3 minutes. Add the Sofrito and nigella seeds, and sauté for 3 minutes, until fragrant. Add the carrots, chicken, and wine. Lower the heat, cover the pan, and allow the mixture to simmer for 5 to 10 minutes, until most of the wine has evaporated. Remove the mixture from the pan and let it cool. Then mix in the cilantro with a fork.

pie filling

¼ cup olive oil

4 Thai bird chiles, sliced

½ cup chopped onion

¼ cup Sofrito (page 240)

2 teaspoons nigella seeds
(see Cook's Note)

8 baby carrots, sliced into ¼-inch-
thick rounds

1 pound roasted chicken meat,
shredded

¼ cup dry white wine

1 bunch fresh cilantro, chopped

Nonstick cooking spray

1 egg yolk

1 teaspoon water

1 teaspoon coarse sea salt

To assemble the meat pies, preheat the oven to 350°F. Lightly spray 8 to 10 cups of two standard muffin tins with nonstick cooking spray.

Roll out the dough on a lightly floured surface to about ⅛-inch thickness and cut out individual rounds using a cookie cutter or the rim of a glass that is larger than the diameter of a muffin cup; you should get about 20 rounds. Lay each round in a muffin cup, and using a pastry brush, brush the edges with water. Fill each dough cup with about 2 tablespoons of the meat filling. Top each one with a second dough round, and seal the edges with a fork.

Whisk the egg yolk with the 1 teaspoon water to create an egg wash. Brush the tops with the egg wash and sprinkle with sea salt.

Bake for 20 minutes or until the tops and bottoms of the pies are golden brown; check by removing one pie from the tin. Transfer the meat pies to a wire rack to cool.

COOK'S NOTE | *Nigella seeds are available at specialty groceries and are often referred to as black cumin; they taste like a combination of onions, black pepper, and oregano. If you cannot find them for this recipe, just replace them with ¼ teaspoon ground cumin.*

RICE, ZUCCHINI, AND FETA FRITTATA WITH FENNEL POLLEN YOGURT

SERVES 6

The textures and flavors in this frittata will win you over, and it is wonderfully satisfying for a picnic. You may also experiment with any combination of cheese, greens, and starch—even leftover pasta works well.

2 tablespoons unsalted butter

2 tablespoons olive oil

10 baby zucchini, sliced lengthwise

4 scallions, sliced

1 cup cooked white rice

½ cup chopped fresh mint

2 tablespoons chopped fresh dill

¾ teaspoon salt

¼ teaspoon freshly ground black pepper

6 eggs

¼ cup heavy cream

¾ cup crumbled feta cheese

Fennel Pollen Yogurt (recipe follows), for serving

Preheat the oven to 400°F.

Heat the butter and oil in a cast-iron skillet over medium-high heat. Add the zucchini and scallions, and sauté until soft. Mix in the rice, mint, and dill, and season with half of the salt and pepper.

In a separate bowl, whisk the eggs, cream, and remaining salt and pepper. Pour over the rice mixture, and cook without stirring for 3 minutes. Sprinkle the crumbled feta on top.

Transfer the skillet to the oven, and bake for 12 to 15 minutes, until golden. Serve with the Fennel Pollen Yogurt.

FENNEL POLLEN YOGURT

MAKES ABOUT 1 CUP

1 cup plain Greek yogurt

2 pinches fennel pollen

2 tablespoons olive oil

Salt and freshly ground black pepper to taste

In a small bowl, whisk together the yogurt, fennel pollen, and olive oil. Season with salt and pepper to taste. Cover and refrigerate for 1 hour to allow the fennel pollen to release its flavor and aroma. Yogurt will keep for 3 days in the refrigerator.

BURRATA SALAD WITH SPICY CAULIFLOWER RELISH AND CROSTINI

SERVES 4 TO 8

Burrata, "buttered" in Italian, is a decadent version of the well-known mozzarella. The exterior is a firm mozzarella shell, while the inside is a splendid ooze of mozzarella and cream. A layered approach to salads is a favorite of ours; it makes the dish easy to transport and unites the flavors in seemingly endless perfect bites.

---

2 large ripe red tomatoes, each sliced into 4 rounds

2 balls Burrata or buffalo mozzarella, each sliced into 4 rounds

Cauliflower Relish (recipe follows)

Plain crostini (see page 216)

Use eight 8-ounce Weck or Mason canning jars for portioning. In each jar, layer the ingredients as follows: 1 slice of tomato, 1 slice of Burrata, and then a couple heaping spoonfuls of the cauliflower relish. Repeat the layers to fill the jar, and seal the top.

Serve the salad with the crostini alongside.

CAULIFLOWER RELISH

MAKES 3 CUPS

1 head cauliflower, cut into florets

¼ cup olive oil

4 Thai bird chiles

2 cloves garlic, finely diced

2 anchovies

8 sprigs fresh thyme

2 teaspoons coarsely ground black pepper, or more to taste

1 red bell pepper, finely diced

1 cup finely diced red onion

2 bay leaves

Salt to taste

¼ cup white balsamic vinegar

1 teaspoon grated fresh ginger (a Microplane works best)

Fresh lemon juice to taste

1 tablespoon chopped fresh dill

Bring a pot of water to a boil. Set out a bowl of ice water.

Add the cauliflower to the boiling water and cook for 7 to 10 minutes, until tender. Using a slotted spoon, transfer the cauliflower to the ice bath for 5 minutes. Cool and drain.

Heat the olive oil in a large skillet over medium-high heat. Add the chiles, garlic, and anchovies, and cook until the anchovies melt, 2 to 3 minutes.

Add the thyme, black pepper, bell pepper, red onion, and bay leaves, and sauté until the onion is tender, 5 minutes. Add the cauliflower and season with salt. Transfer the mixture to a bowl. Remove the chiles, thyme, and bay leaves.

Add the vinegar to the same pot (now dry) you used for the cauliflower. Bring to a boil and cook until the vinegar has reduced by half, 5 minutes. Add the reduced vinegar, the ginger, and the lemon juice to the cauliflower, and toss well.

Add the dill, and season with salt and pepper to taste. Refrigerate the relish for 1 day to allow all the flavors to come together. (The relish will keep in the refrigerator for about 3 days.)

FENNEL SLAW WITH PICKLED RED ONIONS, RAISINS, HAZELNUTS, AND MINT

SERVES 4 TO 6

Fennel is a wonderful alternative to the standard cabbage in this slaw. Here it is accentuated by the marriage of sweet, savory, and tart. We filled a one-quart canning jar and brought it in tow.

¼ cup golden raisins

½ cup Pickled Red Onions (page 129), drained

4 cups thinly sliced fennel (preferably sliced on a mandoline)

Juice of ½ lemon

¼ cup olive oil

Sea salt and freshly ground black pepper to taste

¼ cup toasted hazelnuts, coarsely chopped

¼ cup coarsely chopped fresh mint

Place the raisins in a bowl and add water to cover. Set aside to soften and plump up, 15 to 20 minutes.

To keep the pickled red onions from bleeding and discoloring the other components, they should form the first layer in this slaw. Arrange the pickled onions in the bottom of the jar. Drain the raisins and scatter them over the onions. Top with a layer of fennel over the raisins, and season the fennel with the lemon juice, olive oil, sea salt, and pepper. Top with the hazelnuts and mint.

TOMATO AND CANTALOUPE SALAD

SERVES 4 TO 6

An unlikely combination, this salad of tomato and cantaloupe is summer in a jar—with a little kick for fun. One could certainly use a red beefsteak or other variety of tomato.

2 cups cubed ripe green tomato (¾-inch cubes)

2 cups cubed cantaloupe (¾-inch cubes)

1 tablespoon mustard seed oil, or more to taste

¼ teaspoon salt

Juice of ½ lemon

Mix the tomatoes, cantaloupe, mustard seed oil, salt, and lemon juice together in a bowl. Taste, and adjust the seasonings if necessary (if you like, add a little more mustard seed oil so the spice is more pronounced). Play around with the flavors to suit your preference.

| TAQUERIA

MY HUSBAND AND I GOT MARRIED in a small town on the eastern coast of Mexico, joined by a group of our closest and dearest to celebrate our love and commitment. This town has become a home, a place we visit frequently and where we feel truly at ease. When we are in New York, we keep a piece of Mexico close to our hearts by recreating meals inspired by our travels. This meal is festive and bright and not too much of an undertaking. We invite friends over for tacos quite often; we also make them at home just for us. It is an easy meal and is great for communal cooking.

MENU

FISH TACOS WITH AVOCADO CREMA

TORTILLA SOUP

PICKLED RED ONIONS

GUACAMOLE

PICO DE GALLO

SEA SALT CHELADA

CHOCOLATE AND TEQUILA

For the table setting, handmade ceramics and layered fabrics
create a nice atmosphere—feel free to mix and match. We offer generous
taco toppings and lots of cheladas—it's always a merry meal. Make sure to
end the night with sips of tequila and a bit of chocolate for sweetness.

Mission District, San Francisco

FISH TACOS WITH AVOCADO CREMA

SERVES 6 TO 8

This is a lighter version of the traditional fried-fish taco. A great-quality fish works well here.

1 pound fresh halibut fillet (or other market-fresh white fish)

Salt and freshly ground black pepper

4 tablespoons olive oil

3 cloves garlic, smashed

1 small bunch fresh cilantro: whole leaves plus chopped leaves for garnish

Juice of 1 lime

18 to 24 small flour tortillas

Avocado Crema (recipe follows)

Pickled Red Onions (page 129)

Crumbled Cotija cheese

Lime wedges, for serving

Season the fish generously with salt and pepper. Place the fish in a shallow bowl, and add 3 tablespoons of the olive oil, the garlic, whole cilantro leaves, and lime juice. Marinate for 10 to 15 minutes.

Heat a skillet over medium-high heat and add the remaining 1 tablespoon olive oil. Once the oil is hot, add the fish and the liquid from the marinade (discard the garlic and cilantro leaves). Fry the fish for 3 to 4 minutes on each side. Transfer to a serving platter or board, season with salt and pepper, and top with the chopped cilantro.

Using tongs, hold each tortilla a few inches above a gas flame to create a charred edge.

To serve, lay a tortilla on a plate, add a small portion of fish, and top it with Pickled Red Onions, Avocado Crema, and Cotija cheese. Serve with a wedge of lime.

AVOCADO CREMA

MAKES ABOUT ⅔ CUP

This recipe comes from a sweet man at a small grocery shop in Mexico. The cilantro adds that extra bit of freshness, and if you can find authentic Mexican crema, it will be worth the search.

½ avocado

5 tablespoons Mexican crema (or use crème fraîche)

Juice of ½ lime

¼ cup chopped fresh cilantro

½ teaspoon salt

Combine the avocado, crema, lime juice, cilantro, and salt in a blender and blend on medium-high speed until smooth.

TORTILLA SOUP

SERVES 6 TO 8

Start your dinner preparations by putting this on the stove first. It takes more than an hour for the ingredients to meld, allowing you the time to create the rest of the meal.

---

soup

3 tablespoons vegetable oil

1 large onion, chopped

3 cloves garlic, chopped

1 poblano chile

½ teaspoon salt

Freshly ground black pepper to taste

Juice of ½ lime

¼ teaspoon ground cumin

½ teaspoon smoked paprika

½ teaspoon ground coriander

2 bay leaves

1 teaspoon crushed red pepper flakes

¼ cup fresh cilantro leaves, chopped

One 32-ounce can crushed tomatoes

Two 32-ounce boxes chicken stock

toppings

1 cup vegetable oil

4 small corn tortillas, cut into thin strips

¼ avocado, diced

¼ onion, diced

¼ cup crumbled Cotija cheese

Lime wedges

Chopped fresh cilantro

Sliced radishes

Make the soup: In a large Dutch oven or heavy saucepan, heat the vegetable oil over high heat. Add the onion, garlic, poblano chile, salt, and black pepper. Reduce the heat to medium and sauté for about 2 minutes. Then add the lime juice, cumin, paprika, coriander, bay leaves, red pepper flakes, and cilantro. Continue to cook for 2 to 3 minutes, until the seasonings release their aromas and the onion and chile have softened.

Add the tomatoes and chicken stock, and bring to a boil over high heat. Then reduce the heat to medium, cover the pan halfway, and cook, stirring intermittently, for about 1½ hours.

While the soup is cooking, prepare the tortilla strips: Heat the vegetable oil in a small saucepan over high heat. Fry the tortilla strips in the hot oil for about 3 minutes, until crisp. Remove with a slotted spoon and drain on paper towels.

Once the liquid has thickened, remove the bay leaves and puree the soup with an immersion blender. If you do not have an immersion blender you may puree it in batches in a professional blender (carefully, as the liquid will be quite hot).

Serve the soup in bowls with the tortilla strips, avocado, onion, cheese, lime wedges, cilantro, and radishes as toppings.

PICKLED RED ONIONS

MAKES 1 CUP

A brightly colored garnish, these pickled onions add to the balance of flavor and texture. Try them on sandwiches and in salads.

1½ cups white wine vinegar

¼ cup sugar

½ teaspoon salt

1 bay leaf

1 small dried chile pepper

1 large red onion, sliced into thin rings

In a small nonreactive saucepan, combine the vinegar, sugar, salt, bay leaf, and dried chile and bring to a boil. Add the onion slices, lower the heat, and simmer gently for 30 seconds. Remove from the heat and let cool completely.

Transfer the onions and the liquid to a jar and refrigerate until ready to use. They will keep for a few weeks refrigerated.

GUACAMOLE

MAKES 4 CUPS

This is a straightforward guacamole. We like it pretty tart, but you should feel free to reduce the lime juice to your taste. We also add olive oil, which is not traditional but gives the guacamole a creamy, full-bodied finish. Serve it with your favorite tortilla chips.

½ large onion, chopped small

Juice of 2 limes

½ teaspoon salt

5 avocados

1 tablespoon olive oil

1 tablespoon chopped fresh cilantro

1 teaspoon garlic powder

1 teaspoon onion powder

Combine the onion, lime juice, and salt in a wide, shallow bowl and allow to marinate while you peel and pit the avocados.

Add the avocados to the bowl and smash until they are mashed but still slightly chunky. Then add the olive oil, cilantro, garlic powder, and onion powder. Stir well, taste, and add more salt if desired.

PICO DE GALLO

MAKES ABOUT 2½ CUPS

Made with fresh tomatoes, this salsa is the classic topping for any taco, soup, or sandwich. Add the jalapeño if you like your pico de gallo to be spicy.

½ medium onion, diced

Juice of 2 limes

2 medium tomatoes, diced (about 2 cups)

1 tablespoon diced jalapeño (optional)

¼ cup fresh cilantro, chopped

1 tablespoon olive oil

Coarse salt to taste

Combine the onion and lime juice in a medium bowl and allow to marinate while you prepare the remaining ingredients.

Add the tomatoes, jalapeño if using, cilantro, olive oil, and salt to the onion, and toss to combine.

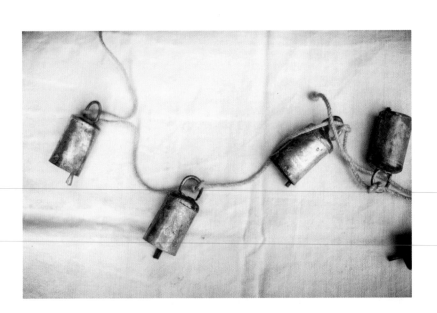

SEA SALT CHELADA

SERVES 1

This refreshing beverage is prepared with an abundance of lime juice (more than you would think). Rim your glass with a nice sea salt, pour a light beer over the lime juice, and enjoy.

Coarse sea salt

Ice cubes

Juice of 2 limes

One 12-ounce bottle light beer
(Corona works well)

Scatter coarse sea salt on a small plate. Wet the rim of a tall glass with cold water, and dip the rim in the salt. Fill the glass with ice cubes and add the lime juice. Top with the beer, and enjoy.

COOK'S NOTE | Michelada *or* Cerveza preparada *(a prepared beer) is a term for beer traditionally mixed with lime juice, tomato juice, and hot sauce or salsa. It is native to Mexico and was first prepared in the 1940s. Add a dash of Tabasco or hot sauce to this recipe if you prefer the spice.*

BIRTHDAYS FOR
LITTLE ONES

MOTHERHOOD HAS TAUGHT ME MANY LESSONS, the elusiveness of time being one of them. As my daughter, Sophia, grows older I have learned to savor the present. I hold clear memories of the day she was born, and am surprised at the realization that she is now two—a little person with charm and a sense of humor. She loves owls, books, olives, and rain boots and surprises me with quirky statements like "Hey mama" and grown-up words like "archaeologists." I am astonished at her growth every single day.

When I reflect on my own childhood, I come up with piece-like memories: flashes frozen in time yet permanently etched in my mind. As Sophia grows, creating and celebrating moments is the greatest form of time spent. I am not sure which of these morsels Sophia will collect in her treasure of memories, but I hope to create many special days for her to choose from.

MENU

BEEF AND GREEN OLIVE EMPANADAS

BLACK BEANS AND RICE

MIXED ROOT VEGETABLE CHIPS

RICOTTA FRITTERS WITH GRAPE JAM

CHOCOLATE CAKE WITH WHITE ICING

FOR FUN

HOORAY SIGN, HAND-PAINTED

POLAROID CAMERAS AND FILM

DESIGN STATION: ANIMAL MASKS

CLEAR BALLOONS FILLED WITH CONFETTI

OWL MUGS

PINK CAKE FLAGS

This party is a modest affair—meant for the kiddos but with thought given to the parents and chaperones. For these types of gatherings we favor finger foods and self-serve options that allow adult guests to mingle while still keeping a watchful eye on their little ones.

Sunday Suppers Studio
Brooklyn, New York

BEEF AND GREEN OLIVE EMPANADAS

MAKES 15 TO 20

These handheld pockets are stuffed with a flavorful filling and feature a flaky exterior. No plates needed—just serve with napkins.

---

empanada dough

3¾ cups all-purpose flour, plus extra for dusting

1 tablespoon sugar

1¾ teaspoons salt

20 twists of a pepper mill

12 tablespoons (1½ sticks) cold unsalted butter, cut into cubes

1¼ cups ice-cold water

beef and olive filling

½ tablespoon olive oil

1 medium onion, cut into small dice

2 cloves garlic, chopped

1 pound ground grass-fed beef

½ teaspoon salt

Pinch of freshly ground black pepper

¼ teaspoon ground cumin

¼ cup dry white wine

¼ cup fresh cilantro leaves, chopped

½ cup pimiento-stuffed olives, sliced

¾ cup tomato sauce

Vegetable oil, for deep frying

Prepare the dough: Combine the flour, sugar, salt, and pepper in a food processor and mix well. Add the butter and pulse until the mixture forms pea-size pieces. Working with ¼ cup of the ice water at a time, add water while pulsing the processor, stopping once the dough comes together and can be formed into a ball. Set the dough onto a piece of plastic wrap, flatten it into a thick disk, and wrap it up. Allow the dough to rest in the refrigerator for at least 2 hours. (The dough will keep in the refrigerator for up to 1 week or in the freezer for a few months.)

Make the filling: Heat the olive oil in a large sauté pan over medium heat. Add the onion and garlic, and cook for 2 to 3 minutes, until the onion is translucent and fragrant but not browned. Add the beef, salt, pepper, and cumin and cook for 3 to 4 minutes, until the beef is lightly browned.

Add the wine, cilantro, olives, and tomato sauce and cook over medium heat for 7 minutes, stirring often. Remove from the heat and allow the filling to cool completely.

Remove any excess fat from the surface of the cooled filling, using a small spoon.

On a lightly floured surface divide the dough into four sections and roll each one out to ⅛-inch thickness. Using a 4½-inch round cookie or biscuit cutter, cut out 12 rounds. Spoon 1 tablespoon of the filling onto each dough round. Fold each disk in half and crimp the edges together with a fork or by folding small segments over the other in an overlapping manner, pinching down as you go.

Pour enough vegetable oil into a large, deep frying pan to cover the empanadas by about 2 inches. Heat the oil until it registers 360° to 375°F on a deep-frying thermometer. Working in batches, fry the empanadas in the hot oil until the crusts are golden brown, occasionally turning them over and spooning the hot oil over the tops. Drain on paper towels and serve warm.

BLACK BEANS AND RICE

SERVES 6

You cannot go wrong with homemade rice and beans; filling and wholesome, it is a weeknight staple in our home.

---

beans

2½ cups dried black beans

2 tablespoons olive oil

1 onion, chopped

3 cloves garlic, chopped

1 bay leaf

9 cups chicken stock

1 tablespoon red wine vinegar

Salt and freshly ground black pepper to taste

rice

2 tablespoons canola oil

2 cups long-grain white rice

4 cups water

1 teaspoon kosher salt

Pinch of freshly ground black pepper

Chopped fresh cilantro, for garnish (optional)

Crumbled Cotija cheese, for garnish (optional)

Rinse the beans in a colander under running water, put them in a large bowl, and add water to cover. Soak overnight.

Heat the olive oil in a large pot or Dutch oven over medium-high heat. Add the onion and garlic, and cook until the onion is translucent and fragrant, 3 to 5 minutes. Drain the beans and add them to the pot, along with the bay leaf and chicken stock. Bring to a boil. Add the vinegar, and season with salt and pepper to taste. Cover and simmer over low heat, stirring occasionally, until the beans are tender, 30 to 45 minutes. Remove the bay leaf. (If you prefer a thicker consistency for the beans, remove about 1 cup of beans and puree them in a blender. Return this puree to the pot and stir it in.)

While the beans are cooking, prepare the rice: Heat the oil in a small pot. Add the rice and toast for 2 minutes, stirring constantly so it doesn't burn. Add the water, kosher salt, and pepper; stir once and bring to a simmer. Lower the heat, cover the pot, and simmer for 20 minutes, until the water has evaporated. Avoid lifting the lid during this time. Remove from the heat and allow the rice to sit, covered, for 5 to 10 minutes. Fluff with a fork before serving.

Serve the beans over the rice, topped with a sprinkle of chopped cilantro and Cotija cheese, if desired.

COOK'S NOTE | *For a quicker method, you can use canned black beans. The secret to this stew is the red wine vinegar—the bit of tartness does wonders for the flavor.*

MIXED ROOT VEGETABLE CHIPS

SERVES 6

Crunchy baked vegetable chips are a true hit with kids and parents alike. Low-moisture vegetables, like potatoes and beets, work especially well. We played around a bit with color and texture to create this mix. Other root vegetables to try: lotus root and parsnip.

1 sweet potato, peeled

1 white sweet potato, peeled

2 golden beets, peeled

2 Chioggia beets, peeled

Kosher salt

Preheat the oven to 250°F. Line two rimmed baking sheets with paper towels.

Slice the sweet potatoes and beets very thin on a mandoline or with a handheld slicer. Arrange the slices on the prepared baking sheets and season with kosher salt. Allow them to sweat for 30 minutes. As the salt extracts the moisture of the vegetables, pat the slices dry with fresh paper towels.

Line a baking sheet with parchment paper and arrange the slices in one layer. Bake for 1 to 1½ hours, until crispy.

COOK'S NOTE | *The Chioggia beet is a pre-1840 heirloom variety, originally from the Italian coastal town of Chioggia. The skin is a fuchsia color, and when sliced open, the inside has beautiful pink and white stripes. The flesh is very tender, mild, and sweet.*

RICOTTA FRITTERS WITH GRAPE JAM

MAKES 24

Warm and fluffy, these lovely fried treats are delightful. The jam can be made with other ripe fruit, such as plums, peaches, or cherries.

grape jam
2 pounds very ripe red-fleshed grapes

Pinch of granulated sugar, if needed

fritters
2 quarts vegetable oil, for frying

1½ cups all-purpose flour

1 tablespoon baking powder

1 teaspoon kosher salt

4 eggs, lightly beaten

¼ cup granulated sugar

2 teaspoons grated orange zest

Seeds from 1 vanilla bean

2 cups ricotta

Confectioners' sugar or granulated sugar, for dusting

Make the jam: In a fine-mesh strainer set over a bowl, pull open the skins of the grapes to expose the flesh. Holding the skins, press the flesh against the strainer to extract the juice and allow it to drain into the bowl. Discard the skins and seeds. Use as is, or season the juice with a tiny pinch of sugar if needed. Refrigerate, covered, until ready to use, up to 1 day.

Make the fritters: In a wide medium stockpot, Dutch oven, or deep fryer, heat the oil until it registers 365°F on a deep-frying thermometer.

Meanwhile, in a bowl, whisk together the flour, baking powder, and kosher salt. In a separate bowl, whisk together the eggs, granulated sugar, orange zest, vanilla seeds, and ricotta. Whisk the dry ingredients into the wet just until incorporated. (The batter can be stored, covered, in the refrigerator for several hours or up to 1 day.)

Working in batches of about 8, gently drop 1-tablespoon balls of the batter into the hot oil and fry, turning them occasionally, until golden all over, about 3 minutes per batch. Using a slotted spoon, transfer the fritters to paper towels to drain. (Allow the oil come back to temperature between batches.)

Sprinkle the fritters with confectioners' sugar or coat them with granulated sugar. Serve warm with the grape jam.

CHOCOLATE CAKE WITH WHITE ICING

MAKES 12 MINI BUNDT CAKES OR 1 LARGE BUNDT CAKE

This cake is vegan, though one would never know it. It is moist and delicate, with just the right lightness. To serve, be playful with heights and stands for mini cakes; we used cooling racks and added a few cake flags for color.

¼ cup unsweetened cocoa powder, plus extra for dusting

1½ cups all-purpose flour

1¼ cups sugar

1 teaspoon baking soda

½ teaspoon salt

⅓ cup vegetable oil

1 teaspoon vanilla extract

1 teaspoon distilled white vinegar

1¼ cups water

White Icing (recipe follows)

Preheat the oven to 350°F. Lightly grease 12 mini Bundt pans or one 10-inch Bundt pan, and dust with cocoa powder.

In a large bowl, sift together the flour, sugar, cocoa powder, baking soda, and salt.

In a medium bowl, combine the oil, vanilla, vinegar, and water and mix until smooth. Add the wet ingredients to the dry, and whisk until smooth.

Pour the batter into the prepared cake pans, filling them three-quarters of the way full. Bake mini cakes for 20 to 25 minutes, a larger cake for about 45 minutes, until a tester inserted into the center comes out clean. Remove from the oven and allow to cool in the pans on a rack. Once cooled, transfer the cakes onto platters or cake stands. Drizzle the icing over the cooled cakes.

WHITE ICING

MAKES 2 CUPS

4½ cups confectioners' sugar

¼ cup water, plus more if needed

In a bowl, whisk together the confectioners' sugar and water until smooth. If the icing is too thick, add more water, 1 teaspoon at a time. Use immediately.

WHISKEY
FEAST

WE LOVE TO GATHER IN UNEXPECTED LOCALES. This meal is set in the historic Brooklyn Navy Yard, at the Kings County Distillery (one of the oldest operating whiskey distilleries in New York City). The menu is a hefty one, meant to satisfy the hungriest of gentlemen. We pack a deck of cards and have plenty of whiskey on hand, as this type of merriment can go on for hours.

KINGS COUNTY DISTILLERY
chocolate "flavored" whiskey
40% alcohol by volume, 375ml

MENU

WHISKEY-GLAZED RIBS

CHILI, TEXAS STYLE

THICK-CUT FRIES WITH PINK
PEPPERCORN AIOLI

WINTER SLAW

CUCUMBER DILL PICKLES

DATE CAKE WITH TOFFEE SAUCE

This meal, prepared at our loft and brought over
in travel ware, is mostly served at room temperature.
The rest we simply reheat on a hot plate.

Kings County Distillery
Brooklyn, New York

WHISKEY-GLAZED RIBS

SERVES 6

This is a generously portioned recipe—these ribs tend to disappear quickly. Sleeves should be rolled up—use your hands and enjoy. A good-quality whiskey goes a long way.

marinade and glaze

1 teaspoon cumin seeds

½ teaspoon coriander seeds

One and a half 32-ounce cans tomato sauce (about 48 ounces)

4 cups light brown sugar

2 cups ketchup

2 cups cider vinegar

2 cups whiskey

1 cup Worcestershire sauce

1 cup soy sauce

4 teaspoons salt

4 racks baby back ribs

Toast the cumin and coriander seeds in a dry skillet over medium heat until fragrant, about 1 minute. Transfer to a mortar and pestle and crush together until fine.

In a large bowl, combine the crushed spices with the tomato sauce, brown sugar, ketchup, vinegar, whiskey, Worcestershire, soy sauce, and salt. Mix well.

Place the ribs in a roasting pan or on a large rimmed baking sheet. Pour the mixture over the ribs, cover with plastic wrap, and marinate in the refrigerator overnight.

Remove the ribs from the refrigerator and allow them to come to room temperature; this will take a few hours.

Preheat the oven 325°F.

If necessary, transfer the ribs and marinade to a baking pan that is big enough so the racks lie flat in a single layer. Cover with foil and bake, basting occasionally, until fork-tender, about 3 hours.

Remove the ribs from the marinade and set them aside. Transfer the marinade to a saucepan and cook over medium-high heat until it becomes a glaze, about 15 minutes. Set aside.

Preheat the broiler or grill.

Glaze the ribs with the reduced marinade. Place them on a rimmed baking sheet and broil them in the broiler, or cook them directly on the grill, for about 5 minutes, until slightly charred.

CHILI, TEXAS STYLE

SERVES 6

Cooking this chili for hours over a medium flame results in tender meat and a good marriage of flavors. It has quite a kick, but unlike traditional Texas chili, our version uses beans. Feel free to taste as you cook and add more spice as desired.

---

3 dried ancho, New Mexico red, or guajillo chiles, seeds removed

2 tablespoons chipotles in adobo sauce (about one-third of a 7-ounce can), chopped

Boiling water

1½ pounds beef chuck, cubed

Salt and freshly ground black pepper

1 tablespoon canola oil

1 large onion, diced

6 cloves garlic, minced

1 tablespoon dried oregano

1 teaspoon ground cumin

1 teaspoon ground coriander

One 32-ounce can chopped tomatoes

One 16-ounce can tomato sauce

1 tablespoon sugar

One 16-ounce can cranberry beans, rinsed and drained

Place the ancho chiles and chipotles in a blender and add enough boiling water to cover them completely. Allow them to soften in the water for 15 minutes. Then puree until smooth. Set aside.

Season the meat with salt and pepper. In a large pot or Dutch oven, heat the canola oil over medium-high heat. Add the meat and sear until browned, 3 to 5 minutes.

Add the onion and garlic to the pot and sauté over low to medium heat until tender, about 5 minutes Add the oregano, cumin, and coriander, and sauté for an additional minute. Stir in the tomatoes, tomato sauce, chile puree, and sugar.

Simmer the chili, partially covered, over medium heat for 3 to 4 hours, until the meat is fork-tender. Add the beans and simmer for an additional 20 minutes.

THICK-CUT FRIES WITH PINK PEPPERCORN AIOLI

SERVES 6

Double frying yields a crispy exterior and a soft inside. We favor a baking potato like the Idaho because its proportion of starch is best for frying. The peppercorn aioli makes a great dipping sauce.

5 pounds baking potatoes, cut into thick fries

pink peppercorn aioli
4 cloves garlic

4 large egg yolks

Juice of 1 lemon, plus more to taste

1 teaspoon salt, plus more to taste

1 cup extra virgin olive oil

1 cup canola or grapeseed oil

2 teaspoons pink peppercorns, crushed

Vegetable oil, for deep frying

Sea salt, for serving

Place the potatoes in a pot of heavily salted cold water. Bring to almost a boil. Once you see the first big bubble of a boil, remove the potatoes. They should be cooked but not falling apart. Drain and rinse under cool water.

Place the potatoes on a wire rack set over a baking sheet, and chill in the refrigerator for about 1 hour.

Make the aioli: Combine the garlic, egg yolks, lemon juice, and salt in a food processor and process until smooth, about 30 seconds. With the motor running, add both oils in a slow, steady stream. If the aioli becomes too thick, thin it with a tablespoon of water. Add the peppercorns and process for a few seconds.

Adjust the seasoning as needed with more salt and/or lemon juice to taste.

In a wide medium stockpot, Dutch oven, or deep fryer, heat the oil until it registers 325°F on a deep-frying thermometer. Working in batches, deep-fry the potatoes until a crust forms but before they begin to show any color.

Using a slotted spoon, transfer the fries to a paper-towel-lined baking sheet and let them cool in the refrigerator.

Reheat the oil to 385°F, and working in batches, fry the potatoes one last time until golden and crispy. Drain on paper towels.

Serve warm, seasoned with sea salt and a generous helping of aioli.

WINTER SLAW

SERVES 6

This slaw draws upon the beautiful colors and textures at the winter market. Take the liberty to create your own, using varieties of cabbage, apples, and even nuts.

1 cup Pink Peppercorn Aioli (page 158)

1 tablespoon white wine vinegar

Grated zest and juice of 2 limes

Salt and freshly ground black pepper

¼ white cabbage

½ medium purple cabbage

¼ large daikon radish, julienned

1 bunch Lacinato kale, shredded

1 yellow carrot, julienned

1 orange carrot, julienned

½ cup torn fresh mint leaves

In a large bowl, whisk together the aioli, vinegar, and lime zest and juice. Season with salt and pepper to taste. Shred the cabbages and add to the bowl of dressing along with the radish, kale, and carrots. Toss to combine. Refrigerate, covered, for 1 hour.

Just before serving, toss in the mint and season with more salt and pepper if necessary.

CUCUMBER DILL PICKLES

MAKES ONE 12-OUNCE JAR

This is a quick pickle that retains the color and crispness of the cucumber. It's a universal recipe that can be used for many other fruits and vegetables; try carrots, beets, and turnips.

3 cups distilled white vinegar

½ cup sugar

2 teaspoons coarse salt

½ teaspoon mustard seeds

1 jalapeño or Thai bird chile

1 large cucumber, sliced in rounds

1½ cups small fresh dill fronds

In a small saucepan, combine the vinegar, sugar, salt, mustard seeds, and chile, sliced in half lengthwise, and bring to a boil. Remove from the heat and refrigerate until cool, about 2 hours.

Arrange the cucumber and the dill in a 12-ounce canning jar. Pour the brine into the jar to completely cover the cucumber, and seal. Refrigerate until cool, about 2 hours. (Will keep refrigerated for up to 1 week.)

DATE CAKE WITH TOFFEE SAUCE

SERVES 6 TO 8

This cake was inspired by a dessert at Moto, a tiny restaurant located under an elevated subway line in Brooklyn. Served warm, it is moist and decadent and may redefine dessert for you. This is our version, which comes amazingly close to the original.

---

cake

¾ pound dried dates, pitted and finely chopped

2¼ cups water

1½ teaspoons baking soda

8 tablespoons (1 stick) unsalted butter, melted

¾ cup granulated sugar

2 tablespoons light brown sugar

2 large eggs

1⅔ cups all-purpose flour

sauce

8 tablespoons (1 stick) unsalted butter

1 cup heavy cream

1 cup plus 2 tablespoons light brown sugar

2 teaspoons vanilla extract

Whipped cream, for serving (optional)

Place the dates in a heatproof bowl.

Bring the water to a boil in a saucepan and pour it over the dates. Stir in the baking soda, cover the bowl, and set aside to allow the dates to absorb the water, about 30 minutes.

Meanwhile, preheat the oven to 350°F. Grease a 10-inch square baking pan.

Puree the date mixture in a food processor until smooth.

In a large bowl, combine the melted butter and both sugars. Whisk in the eggs. Stir in the flour and the date puree. Pour the batter into the prepared baking pan, and bake for 50 to 60 minutes. The cake should be moist and a little sticky when a toothpick is inserted into the center.

To make the sauce, combine the butter, cream, brown sugar, and vanilla in a medium saucepan. Whisk over medium heat for about 10 minutes, until the mixture thickens.

Cut the warm cake into squares and drizzle toffee sauce generously over each serving. If desired, add a dollop of whipped cream.

HOLIDAY

THIS DECADENT MEAL IS ONE OF OUR FAVORITES. The table is adorned in jewel tones, mixed and matched. Vessels are humble containers, and can be a pot off the stovetop. The greens and leaves of the season make a beautiful wreath as well as small place cards for guests at the table. An over-flowing buffet allows friends and family to serve themselves. This meal brings together the bounty of the season and allows for lingering and leftovers.

MENU

TRUFFLED TURKEY WITH WHITE WINE GRAVY

WILD MUSHROOM
AND BRIOCHE STUFFING

CRANBERRY-APPLE RELISH

BUTTERED BRUSSELS LEAVES

MASHED POTATOES

SPICED PUMPKIN CRÈME BRÛLÉE

The truffled turkey is extraordinary, and the sides are
equally rich. As far as holiday meals go, this one is not out of reach.
A bit of prep, an organized list, and a little whimsy go a long way.

SHOPPING LIST

Farmers' Market
BRUSSELS SPROUTS

GARLIC

YUKON GOLD POTATOES

SHALLOTS

LEEKS

KING TRUMPET OR
CREMINI MUSHROOMS

THYME

PARSLEY

LEMON

APPLE

CRANBERRIES

BRIOCHE BREAD

Poultry
TURKEY

Dairy
SOUR CREAM

BUTTER

MILK

TRUFFLE BUTTER

COMTÉ OR GRUYÈRE CHEESE

EGGS

HEAVY CREAM

Pantry
WHITE WINE

CHICKEN OR TURKEY STOCK

CINNAMON STICK AND
GROUND CINNAMON

NUTMEG

CANNED PUMPKIN PUREE

VANILLA BEAN

TRUFFLED TURKEY WITH WHITE WINE GRAVY

SERVES 8 TO 10

A truffle- and butter-infused turkey takes holiday indulgence to another level. Inspired by a recipe in *Gourmet* magazine, we have tweaked this recipe and cooked it for many of our Thanksgiving meals. The turkey is moist, golden, and a bit fancy—perfectly suited for a special occasion.

One 14- to 16-pound turkey, neck and giblets removed

2½ teaspoons salt

1½ teaspoons freshly ground black pepper

4 ounces black-truffle butter, at room temperature (see Cook's Note)

6 cups chicken or turkey stock

White Wine Gravy (recipe follows)

Supplies: Kitchen string; 17 × 14-inch flameproof roasting pan with a flat rack

Remove the turkey from refrigeration and allow to come to room temperature for about an hour. Position a rack in the lower third of the oven and preheat the oven to 450°F.

While the oven is heating, rinse the turkey inside and out, and pat it dry. Mix the salt and pepper in a small bowl. Working from the end with the large cavity, carefully run your fingers underneath the skin to loosen it, being mindful not to tear the skin. Rub the truffle butter under as well as over the skin. Sprinkle the salt and pepper mixture evenly in the turkey cavities and all over the skin. Fold the neck skin under the body, tuck the wing tips under the breasts, and tie the drumsticks together with string.

Place the turkey on a rack in a roasting pan, and pour in 2 cups of the stock. Tent with aluminum foil, being careful that the foil does not touch the turkey. Roast for 1 hour.

Remove the aluminum foil and baste the turkey with the juices in the bottom of the roasting pan. Reduce the oven temperature to 375°F and pour 2 cups of the stock into the pan. Roast for 30 minutes.

Add the remaining 2 cups of stock to the pan. Continue to roast, basting the turkey every 30 minutes, until an instant-read thermometer inserted into the thickest part of each thigh (close to but not touching bone) registers 170°F, another 1 to 1½ hours (2½ to 3 hours total).

Remove the pan from the oven and carefully tilt the turkey so the juices from inside the large cavity run into the pan. Transfer the turkey to a platter and let it stand, uncovered, for 30 minutes (the temperature of the thigh meat will rise to 175° to 180°F). Remove and discard the string.

Serve the turkey with the White Wine Gravy.

WHITE WINE GRAVY

½ cup finely chopped shallots

2 cups dry white wine

2 cups chicken or turkey stock

6 tablespoons all-purpose flour

3 ounces black-truffle butter, at room temperature (see Cook's Note)

Salt and freshly ground black pepper

Strain the juices from the pan in which you roasted the turkey through a fine-mesh sieve into a 2-quart measuring cup, and skim off and reserve the fat (or use a fat separator). Straddle the roasting pan across two burners, and heat ¼ cup of the reserved fat over medium heat. Add the shallots and cook, stirring, until golden, about 2 minutes. Add the wine and boil, stirring and scraping up the browned bits, until the mixture has reduced to about 1 cup, 5 to 8 minutes.

Strain the liquid through a fine-mesh sieve into a 2- to 3-quart heavy saucepan. Add the stock and the reserved pan juices and bring to a boil.

Mix the flour with the truffle butter to make a roux, and add this to the boiling juices, whisking until thickened. Simmer, whisking occasionally, for 3 to 5 minutes. Season with salt and pepper.

COOK'S NOTE | *If you can't find truffle butter in your specialty grocery store, make your own: Mix together 7 tablespoons room-temperature unsalted butter, 1¾ teaspoons truffle oil, and a bit of salt. Taste, and add more truffle oil as desired. Refrigerate until ready to use.*

WILD MUSHROOM AND BRIOCHE STUFFING

SERVES 6

Earthy flavors combine with slightly sweet brioche bread to create this beautiful stuffing. One could certainly experiment with other breads: raisin or nut varieties could work well. Our homemade Challah Bread (page 210) would also be an excellent choice.

4 tablespoons (½ stick) unsalted butter, at room temperature, plus extra for the baking dish

2 shallots, minced

4 cups sliced leeks (white and light green parts only, ½-inch-thick slices)

1 pound king trumpet or cremini mushrooms, chopped or sliced

2 cloves garlic, minced

Salt and freshly ground black pepper to taste

½ cup dry white wine

4 sprigs fresh thyme

3 large eggs, lightly beaten

1 cup shredded Comté or Gruyère cheese

6 cups cubed brioche

⅓ cup chopped fresh parsley

1 cup chicken stock, plus more if needed

Preheat the oven to 350°F. Butter a 9 × 13-inch baking dish.

Melt the butter in a large saucepan over medium heat. Add the shallots, leeks, mushrooms, and garlic; season with salt and pepper. Cook, stirring occasionally, until the vegetables have softened, 5 to 10 minutes. Add the wine and thyme sprigs, and cook until the wine has evaporated, 3 to 5 minutes. Transfer to a large bowl and remove the thyme sprigs.

In a large bowl, whisk together the eggs, a generous pinch of salt and pepper, and the cheese. Add the cooked vegetables, brioche, and parsley, and toss to combine. Mix in ½ cup of the stock. Continue to add more stock just until the stuffing is moistened but not wet (there should not be any liquid in the bottom of the bowl). Transfer to the prepared baking dish, cover with buttered aluminum foil, and refrigerate.

When you remove the turkey from the oven and set it aside to rest, place the covered baking dish in the oven and bake until the stuffing is warmed through, 25 to 30 minutes. Then uncover and bake until golden, about 15 minutes.

CRANBERRY-APPLE RELISH

SERVES 6

A bit more rustic than the traditional cranberry sauce, this quick cranberry relish is sweet but retains a nice tartness. It is also quite lovely on buttered toast the following morning.

½ lemon, rind and flesh cut into very small dice

2 cups water

1 apple, peeled, cored, and cut into ½-inch cubes

3 cups fresh cranberries

1 cup sugar

½ teaspoon ground cinnamon

Combine the diced lemon, water, apple cubes, cranberries, sugar, and cinnamon in a saucepan and bring to a boil over high heat. Then reduce the heat to low and partially cover the pan. Simmer gently, stirring occasionally, until the sauce thickens, the apple is tender, and the cranberries have burst, 10 to 15 minutes. Allow to cool before serving, or refrigerate covered.

BUTTERED BRUSSELS LEAVES

SERVES 4 TO 6

Bright and buttery, these Brussels sprouts leaves add a little crispness and healthful greens to the meal.

2 tablespoons unsalted butter

2 cloves garlic, smashed and chopped

3 pints Brussels sprouts, pulled apart into leaves, cores discarded

Heat the butter in a large sauté pan. Add the garlic and cook until barely browned, 1 to 2 minutes. Remove the garlic from the pan and set aside.

Add the Brussels sprouts leaves to the pan and sauté until bright green, about 5 minutes. Add the garlic, toss, and serve.

MASHED POTATOES

SERVES 4 TO 6

This is a once-a-year mashed potato, not for the faint of heart. It is rich and creamy, and its decadence makes it the perfect side for the truffled turkey.

6 pounds Yukon Gold potatoes, peeled and cut into ½-inch dice

1 cup sour cream

1½ cups (3 sticks) unsalted butter, at room temperature

¾ cup whole milk

Kosher salt to taste

Freshly ground white pepper to taste

Bring a large pot of salted water to a boil, add the potatoes, and cook until tender, about 20 minutes. Drain in a colander and let them steam dry, 3 to 4 minutes.

Pass the potatoes through a potato ricer or a food mill into the bowl of a stand electric mixer fitted with the whisk attachment. Add the sour cream, butter, milk, salt, and white pepper. Beat the potatoes on medium speed until smooth and just blended.

(If you do not have a stand mixer, pass the potatoes through a ricer or food mill into a large bowl. Using a handheld electric mixer or a sturdy whisk, beat the potatoes with the other ingredients until smooth.)

Taste, and adjust the seasonings with more salt and white pepper as needed. Serve immediately.

COOK'S NOTE | *Our secret to extra-fluffy potatoes is using a ricer, which prevents the potatoes from becoming overly starchy. Using a whisk or mixer briefly creates the additional smoothness.*

SPICED PUMPKIN CRÈME BRÛLÉE

SERVES 6

Crème brûlée offers a sweet end to a lavish feast. Ours is made with pumpkins and is served communally in a large baking pan for all to enjoy.

½ cup plus 4 teaspoons sugar

5 egg yolks, at room temperature

1½ cups heavy cream

1 cinnamon stick

¼ teaspoon freshly grated nutmeg

1 vanilla bean, split lengthwise and seeds reserved

¾ cup pumpkin puree

Boiling water

Preheat the oven to 325°F.

In a heatproof bowl, whisk together the ½ cup sugar and the egg yolks.

In a saucepan, combine the cream, cinnamon stick, nutmeg, and vanilla seeds and bean, and bring to a simmer over medium heat. Rest a fine-mesh sieve over the bowl containing the egg yolk mixture, and slowly pour the hot cream mixture into the yolk mixture while whisking. Whisk in the pumpkin puree.

Pour the mixture into a 9 × 12-inch baking pan and place it in a larger baking pan. Add boiling water to fill the large pan halfway up the sides of the smaller pan. Cover the pans loosely with aluminum foil, and bake until the custard is just set, about 30 minutes.

Transfer the smaller baking pan to a wire rack and let the custard cool to room temperature. Then refrigerate, covered, for at least 4 hours or up to 3 days.

Just before serving, sprinkle the remaining 4 teaspoons sugar evenly over the surface of the custard. Using a kitchen torch, move the flame continuously over the surface until the sugar melts and browns lightly. Serve immediately.

COOK'S NOTE | *A small kitchen torch is not a costly investment and is worth purchasing for fun projects like this.*

EVENING

AUTUMN
DINNER

ON BRISK FALL DAYS we often go for family walks and outings. We collect leaves and take in the change of seasons. On these autumn days the air is cooler and the colors are vibrant. We slow our pace to enjoy the day. Upon our return home we enjoy a warm meal that is already in the making.

MENU

CORNED BEEF WITH ROOT VEGETABLES

BRAISED PURPLE CABBAGE

SESAME AND SALT PRETZELS WITH
BROWN BEER MUSTARD

APPLE AND OLIVE OIL CAKE

———————————

As autumn is a time for harvesting and gathering we find this
meal to be perfectly suited for an early supper with loved ones.
We celebrate the abundance of the season and make warming meals
as the seasons transition. This hefty autumn supper will leave
you with plenty of leftovers for the week ahead.

Blue Hill Farm, New York

CORNED BEEF WITH ROOT VEGETABLES

SERVES 6

Corning beef takes a bit of time and can be ingredient heavy, but it is a worthwhile undertaking. The beef will corn for five days, and then stew for a few hours. The end result is a bit like Thanksgiving, as the leftovers can be all the fun: try corned beef hash or grilled cheese sandwiches.

brine
1½ cups kosher salt

⅔ cup brown sugar

10 pink or black peppercorns

3 tablespoons curing salt

8 cloves garlic

4 bay leaves

1 teaspoon fennel seeds

2 teaspoons yellow mustard seeds

2 whole cloves

1 cinnamon stick

6 sprigs fresh thyme

2 stalks of celery

2 carrots

½ onion

brisket
One 5-pound beef brisket

6 cloves garlic

2 teaspoons coriander seeds

2 teaspoons yellow mustard seeds

2 whole cloves

1 cinnamon stick

1 bunch fresh thyme sprigs

2 whole celery hearts, cut in half

2 bunches baby turnips

1 bunch baby carrots

Make the brine: Pour 5½ quarts water into a large nonreactive pot, and add the kosher salt, brown sugar, peppercorns, curing salt, garlic, bay leaves, fennel seeds, mustard seeds, cloves, cinnamon stick, thyme sprigs, celery, carrots, and onion. Bring to a boil, stirring well to dissolve the salt and brown sugar. Remove from the heat and set aside to cool completely.

Add the brisket to the brine, weighting it down with a plate so it is submerged. Cover and refrigerate for 5 to 6 days.

Remove the brisket from the pot, discard the brine, and rinse the meat.

Place the brisket in a large stockpot and add 5 quarts water; it should cover the meat by 2 inches. Add the garlic, coriander seeds, mustard seeds, cloves, cinnamon stick, and thyme sprigs, and bring to a boil. Lower the heat to a simmer and cook for 5 to 6 hours, until the meat is fork-tender. Remove the brisket, reserving the liquid, and cut it against the grain into medium-thick slices. Keep warm.

Bring the stock back to a boil. Add the celery to the pot and cook until slightly tender, about 5 minutes. Remove the celery with tongs and repeat with the turnips and carrots, cooking them separately.

Arrange the sliced brisket and the vegetables in large individual bowls. Strain and pour the hot stock over, and serve.

BRAISED PURPLE CABBAGE

SERVES 4 TO 6

The color of this dish is spectacular, and the tart buttery flavor combination is a nice update. It is a great side to many weeknight meals and can be served alongside chicken or fish. Be sure not to overcook the cabbage—it is meant to have a nice bite.

3 tablespoons olive oil

1 clove garlic, minced

1 head purple cabbage, cored and shredded

3 tablespoons white wine vinegar

Salt and freshly ground black pepper to taste

2 tablespoons unsalted butter

Heat the oil in large sauté pan over medium heat. Add the garlic and sauté for 1 to 2 minutes. Reduce the heat to low, add the cabbage, and cover the pan. Cook, stirring frequently, until the cabbage begins to soften, about 5 minutes. Then add the vinegar, and season with salt and pepper. Continue to cook, covered, for 15 minutes.

Add the butter and cook for 5 more minutes, until the cabbage is soft but still retains some texture.

SESAME SALT PRETZELS WITH BROWN BEER MUSTARD

MAKES 12 PRETZELS

1½ cups whole milk

1 tablespoon active dry yeast

1 tablespoon honey

2 teaspoons salt

2½ cups all-purpose flour

Vegetable oil

1 tablespoon cornmeal

⅓ cup baking soda

1 tablespoon salt

1 egg yolk

2 tablespoons whole milk

2 tablespoons sesame seeds

Coarse salt, for sprinkling

Heat the milk in a saucepan until bubbles form around the edges. Let cool. Add the yeast and honey, and pour the mixture into the bowl of a stand mixer fitted with the paddle attachment.

In a medium bowl, stir the salt and flour together. Add half of this mixture to the mixer bowl, incorporating it well. Add the remaining flour mixture and mix for 5 minutes. Change to the dough hook and knead on low-medium speed for 10 minutes. Transfer the dough to an oiled bowl. Cover with plastic wrap and let rest in a warm spot for 1½ hours or until doubled in size.

Position a baking stone or baking sheet on the middle rack of the oven and preheat the oven to 450°F. Line a baking sheet with parchment paper and dust it with the cornmeal.

Divide the dough into 12 equal portions. Using your palms, roll each piece of dough into a long strand (20 inches long). Take each end of a dough strand, twist once or twice, flip the joined ends down, and attach them to the rounded portion.

Bring a large pot of water to a boil. Add the baking soda and salt, and lower the heat to just below a simmer. Gently place the pretzels, two at a time, in the water and cook for 20 seconds. Flip and cook for another 20 seconds. Arrange them on a wire rack to dry.

Mix the egg yolk and the 2 tablespoons milk in a small bowl, and brush the tops of the pretzels with it. Sprinkle with the sesame seeds and coarse salt. Transfer the pretzels to the prepared baking sheet, and place the baking sheet on top of the hot stone in the oven. Bake for 8 to 10 minutes, until golden brown. Cool on a wire rack.

BROWN BEER MUSTARD

MAKES 1 CUP

One of our favorite condiments, this mustard will last forever in your fridge—or double the recipe and make a jar for your neighbors.

⅓ cup cider vinegar

1 tablespoon light brown sugar

⅓ cup stout beer

3 tablespoons yellow mustard seeds

3 tablespoons brown mustard seeds

½ teaspoon salt

¼ teaspoon cracked black pepper

In a small container, combine the vinegar, brown sugar, and beer. Add the yellow and brown mustard seeds, and refrigerate covered overnight.

The following day, add the salt and pepper to the mixture, and pulse in a food processor until the desired consistency is reached.

APPLE AND OLIVE OIL CAKE

SERVES 8 TO 10

Using a good-quality olive oil makes a difference in this cake, which is dense and moist and just the right amount of sweet. It goes well at the end of the meal, but it can also be a nice treat in the morning with a cup of herbal tea.

Butter, for the baking dish

3 large eggs

2½ cups sugar

1½ cups extra virgin olive oil

1½ cups whole milk

Grated zest of ½ lemon

2 cups all-purpose flour, plus extra for the baking dish

1 teaspoon baking powder

¼ teaspoon salt

Juice of ½ lemon

1 medium apple

Preheat the oven to 350°F. Butter and flour a 10-inch spring-form pan, or line a round cake pan with parchment paper.

In a large bowl, whisk together the eggs and sugar. Stir in the olive oil, milk, and lemon zest.

In another bowl, sift together the flour, baking powder, and salt. Slowly add the wet ingredients to the dry, stirring until just blended. Do not overmix. Pour the batter into the prepared cake pan.

Place the lemon juice in a large bowl. Peel the apples, and using a mandoline, thinly slice them, dropping the slices into the lemon juice to prevent browning. Arrange the apple slices on top of the cake batter.

Bake for 40 to 50 minutes, until the cake is golden and a toothpick inserted into the center comes out clean. (The bake time may vary. If the cake needs more time but is browning too quickly, tent it with foil and continue baking.) Cool in the pan before unmolding.

SIDES PARTY,
A POTLUCK

THIS POTLUCK IS A GATHERING of cooking and community, a notion
that is close to our hearts. We come together with friends from afar at a cabin
in the woods for a bit of respite. Over the coming days we hike and laugh, eat
warm meals, and gather around the fireplace, feeling truly lucky to be in such
a wonderful place.

Inspired by our surroundings, our friend Amy creates a centerpiece of
foraged branches and leaves to hang as a novel chandelier over the table. As
the weekend comes to an end, we set out buckets of flowers for guests to create their own take-home bouquets.

MENU

MUSTARD AND PEPPERCORN
ROAST BEEF WITH TOMATO GRAVY

BUTTERMILK CORNBREAD
WITH HONEY BUTTER

SWISS CHARD AND BONE MARROW GRATIN

RADISH SALAD

CHOCOLATE BREAD PUDDING
WITH HOMEMADE CHALLAH

Reviving the potluck of yesteryears, this dinner allows even the busiest of
folks a manageable way to enjoy a home-cooked meal with friends.
A mustard and peppercorn roast is the centerpiece, made by the host.
The sides are contributed by friends and guests.

Klein Residence
Beaver Brook, New York

MUSTARD AND PEPPERCORN ROAST BEEF WITH TOMATO GRAVY

SERVES 6 TO 8

Well-seasoned and perfectly tender, this roast will serve a hungry group and leave you with delectable sandwich-destined leftovers. The tomato gravy is a wonderful addition; using the roasting juices and ripe tomatoes, it adds sweet and savory notes to this dish.

roast

1 tablespoon black peppercorns

One 4-pound boneless beef roast (we used an eye round cut)

2 teaspoons salt

¼ cup olive oil, plus 1 tablespoon for searing

1 teaspoon mustard seeds

2 tablespoons unsalted butter, at room temperature

2 tablespoons Dijon mustard

Crush the black peppercorns to a coarse consistency with a mortar and pestle. Season the beef with half of the crushed peppercorns and the 2 teaspoons salt.

Heat the 1 tablespoon olive oil in a large skillet over medium heat. Sear the beef until it is golden brown on all sides, 3 to 5 minutes. Transfer the beef to a roasting pan and cover it loosely with aluminum foil.

Add the mustard seeds to the remaining pepper in the mortar and crush lightly. Add the ¼ cup olive oil, the butter, and the Dijon mustard, and mix well. Coat the beef with this mustard mixture and re-cover with the foil. Allow the beef to marinate in the refrigerator overnight.

About an hour before roasting, remove the beef from the refrigerator to let it come to room temperature.

Preheat the oven to 425°F.

In a bowl, toss the shallots, garlic, and tomatoes with the extra virgin olive oil. Season with salt and pepper to taste, and arrange alongside the beef in the roasting pan.

Roast the beef and vegetables for 20 minutes. Then lower the heat to 350°F and roast for 30 minutes or until the meat is done to your taste. (For medium-rare, remove the roast when an internal temperature of 130°F is reached. If you prefer it more well done, keep the roast in for 10 minutes longer.)

Remove the roast from the pan, cover it with foil, and let it rest in a warm place.

tomato gravy

8 shallots

6 cloves garlic

2 ripe tomatoes, halved

2 tablespoons extra virgin olive oil

Salt and freshly ground
black pepper to taste

2 tablespoons all-purpose flour

1 cup Madeira wine

2½ cups beef stock

1 tablespoon whole-grain mustard

1 tablespoon Dijon mustard

In the meantime, make the gravy: Strain the pan drippings, including the shallots, garlic, and tomatoes, through a fine-mesh sieve into a medium saucepan. Use a fork to mash the shallots, garlic, and tomatoes through the sieve. Bring the strained mixture to a boil.

Lower the heat to medium and sprinkle the flour over the mixture. Mix well. Add the Madeira and cook until it bubbles; then add the stock and both mustards. Season with salt and pepper to taste, and let simmer for 10 minutes, until thickened.

Thinly slice the roast and serve with the tomato gravy.

COOK'S NOTES | *Roasts that work well include tri-tip, round tip, rump, bottom round, and eye round. Setting the meat aside to rest for at least 15 minutes after roasting allows the juices to settle and the meat to become more tender.*

BUTTERMILK CORNBREAD
WITH HONEY BUTTER

SERVES 6 TO 8

I tend to favor a moist cornbread, served warm and slathered in honey butter. It's that mix of sweet and savory and the little bit of crumble that perfectly accompanies the rest of this robust menu.

---

cornbread

1 cup (2 sticks) unsalted butter, plus extra for the pan

½ cup light brown sugar

¼ cup honey

4 large eggs, at room temperature

2 cups buttermilk

1 teaspoon baking soda

2 cups yellow cornmeal

2 cups all-purpose flour

1 teaspoon salt

honey butter

1 cup (2 sticks) unsalted butter, at room temperature

¼ cup honey

Make the cornbread: Preheat the oven to 375°F. Grease an 8 × 13-inch baking pan.

Melt the butter in a large skillet over medium heat. Stir in the brown sugar and honey remove from the heat. Quickly add the eggs and beat until blended.

Combine the buttermilk with the baking soda, and stir into the pan. Stir in the cornmeal, flour, and salt until well blended and few lumps remain.

Pour the batter into the prepared baking pan and bake for 25 to 30 minutes or until a toothpick inserted into the center comes out clean. Cool in the pan and cut into squares for serving.

Meanwhile, make the honey butter: Mix the butter and honey together in a small bowl until well blended. Serve at room temperature with the cornbread.

SWISS CHARD AND BONE MARROW GRATIN

SERVES 4 TO 6

If you haven't ventured into the world of marrow, we encourage you to do so. It adds a welcome dimension of silkiness and decadence that isn't overly heavy. Spread any leftover marrow on toasted bread and top it with a sprinkling of coarse sea salt.

---

1 pound beef marrow bones

3 bunches Swiss chard, leaves and stems separated, stems cut into ½-inch slices

3 tablespoons unsalted butter

⅓ cup all-purpose flour

2½ cups whole milk

2 teaspoons salt

1 teaspoon Dijon mustard

Fill a pot (one that is large enough to hold the marrow bones) with water, season it well with salt, and bring to a boil. Once the water comes to a boil, add the bones, cover, and reduce the heat. Simmer for 5 to 7 minutes, until the marrow has turned a grayish color and is soft when touched with a knife. Remove the bones, allow them to cool, and then scoop out the marrow. (If you have trouble removing the marrow, place the bone on a cutting board and tap the top of the bone with a spoon to help release the marrow.)

Preheat the oven to 375°F. Grease a 9 × 11-inch baking dish.

Bring a large pot of well-salted water to a boil. Add the Swiss chard stems and cook until tender, 5 to 7 minutes. Use a slotted spoon to remove the stems from the pot and set them aside. Add the leaves to the boiling water and blanch for just 3 seconds. Drain the leaves and set them aside with the stems.

Heat the butter in a large heavy saucepan over medium heat. Once the butter begins to foam, add the flour, mix well, and heat until bubbles form. Then gradually whisk in the milk, and season with the salt and mustard. Bring the sauce to a simmer before removing from the heat.

Add the Swiss chard and bone marrow to the sauce. Mix well.

Pour the mixture into the prepared baking dish, and bake until the top is golden, about 30 minutes.

RADISH SALAD

SERVES 6

A beautiful raw salad brings crunch and color to this wintry menu. Allow the radishes to marinate a bit on the platter; as they soften, the flavors will get more pronounced. We opted for watermelon radishes, but use any that catch your eye at the market.

---

8 small or 4 large radishes

1 tablespoon smoked sea salt

Grated zest and juice of 1 lemon

¼ cup extra virgin olive oil

3 tablespoons chopped toasted walnuts

2 tablespoons chopped fresh parsley

Thinly slice the radishes on a mandoline, and arrange on a platter. Sprinkle the sea salt and lemon zest over them. Drizzle with the lemon juice and olive oil, and garnish with the walnuts and parsley.

CHOCOLATE BREAD PUDDING
WITH HOMEMADE CHALLAH

SERVES 8 TO 10

Day-old bread is best for this pudding, as the slightly stale cubes stand up well to the eggy bath. This dessert gives you the best of many worlds: a soft, rich custard, a semisweet bite of melted chocolate, and the crusty topping we all love. (Of course, loads of butter is the trick to that.) For a homemade challah, I've included my family recipe here.

pudding
5 large eggs

¾ cup sugar

2 cups whole milk

2½ cups heavy cream

4 tablespoons (½ stick) unsalted butter, melted

¼ teaspoon salt

1 tablespoon vanilla extract

6 ounces semisweet chocolate chunks

12 cups 1-inch cubes of challah (from about 2 regular loaves or 3 small loaves; recipe follows)

topping
4 tablespoons (½ stick) unsalted butter, melted

½ teaspoon ground cinnamon

3 tablespoons sugar

Prepare the pudding: In a large bowl, whisk together the eggs and sugar. Add the milk, cream, melted butter, salt, vanilla, and chocolate chunks.

Toss 8 cups of the challah cubes with the custard, making sure all of the cubes are well coated. Transfer the cubes to a 12-inch cast-iron skillet, cover it lightly with plastic wrap, and allow to sit for 20 minutes.

Meanwhile, preheat the oven to 325°F.

Make the topping: Combine the melted butter, cinnamon, and sugar in a small saucepan over medium heat. Mix in the remaining 4 cups of challah. Place these challah cubes on top of the pudding and press down on them to partially submerge the bread (this will become the crispy topping).

Bake for 50 minutes or until set. Serve warm, straight from the skillet.

CHALLAH BREAD

MAKES 2 ROUND LOAVES

As a young girl, I knew the smell of my mother's baked challah signaled the beginning of her Friday-evening preparations. Each week our kitchen would overflow with these beautiful braided breads, some of which we would deliver to friends and family. My mother cooks and bakes in the manner of many grandparents: unscripted and unmeasured. Her consistent result is remarkable to me. After several sessions of testing and retesting, we finally documented the mystery of the beautiful challah of my childhood. This challah is bread-like, dense, soft, and just sweet enough.

3 tablespoons active dry yeast

¾ cup plus 1½ tablespoons sugar

2½ cups warm water (110°F)

10 cups all-purpose flour, plus extra for dusting

¾ cup vegetable oil

1 tablespoon salt

2 eggs: 1 whole, 1 separated

1 teaspoon water

Nonstick cooking spray

In a small bowl, dissolve the yeast and the 1½ tablespoons sugar in 2 cups warm water. Cover and set aside for 10 minutes or until bubbles form.

In the large bowl of a stand mixer fitted with the dough hook, combine the flour, remaining ¾ cup sugar, oil, salt, whole egg, and egg white. Mix on very low speed.

With the mixer running, slowly add the remaining ½ cup warm water and then continue to knead for 5 minutes. The dough should feel soft and not too sticky. Transfer the dough to an oiled bowl, cover it with a towel, and allow it to rest in a warm place for 1 hour or until it has doubled in size.

Punch down the dough, cover it, and let it rise again in a warm place for 30 minutes.

Grease two 8-inch cast-iron pans with nonstick spray.

Turn the dough out onto a lightly floured surface and divide it into 8 equal balls. Roll each ball into a strand about 12 inches long. Place 2 strands horizontally and 2 strands vertically, in the form of a hashtag. Braid the strands, moving from right to left, always taking the strand that is underneath and crossing it over the next strand, moving in a circular motion from right to left until a circle has formed. Tuck the remaining ends under, and place each challah in one of the prepared cast-iron pans.

In a small bowl, beat together the remaining egg yolk and the 1 teaspoon water, and brush the top of each challah. Place the pans in a warm place and allow the challahs to rise again, uncovered, for 1 hour or until doubled in size.

Position a rack in the middle of the oven and preheat the oven to 350°F.

Bake for 35 to 40 minutes, until golden brown. Let cool.

UPSTATE
WITH FRIENDS

THIS MEAL HIGHLIGHTS THE BEAUTY of its ingredients in a straightforward manner. In their simplicity, the textures and flavors linger on your palate. At our table we serve an array of crostini adorned in colorful toppings, a hand-cut pasta, a whole roasted cauliflower, and an ice cream sampler for a bit of freshness and vibrancy.

MENU

ASSORTED CROSTINI

WHOLE ROASTED CAULIFLOWER

MALTAGLIATI WITH WILD MUSHROOMS

ICE CREAM SAMPLER

The table setting is a simple approach, a white surface of neutrals and clay pots. Handwrite your menu on a sheet of large kraft paper to hang on a nearby wall, and use some of the paper for the tabletop as well. Buy fresh breads on the day of, and load the table with white plates and other ceramics. Red wine pairs well with this meal. Here we made our own labels and adhered them to glass jugs with black tape. The table is simple but classic—fit for an Italian feast. Send your guests home with a bag of herbed sea salt, easily assembled and a fun seasoning for all cooks.

Eldred, New York

ASSORTED CROSTINI

SERVES 4 TO 6 (ENOUGH TOAST FOR 1 TOPPING RECIPE, BELOW)

These crostini are a favorite at our summer table. Inspired by a beloved neighborhood restaurant, we pick up fresh bread and a variety of seasonal ingredients, mixing and experimenting along the way. The recipes below are just a guideline; feel free to discover your own flavors. You'll find that the trick is a balance of salt, sweet, texture, and a hit of tart or spice.

---

2 tablespoons extra virgin olive oil

8 slices country loaf, sliced ½-inch thick

1 clove garlic, halved

Topping of choice (recipes follow)

Preheat the oven to 450°F.

Brush the olive oil over one side of each bread slice, and place them in a single layer on a baking sheet. Toast the bread, flipping the slices once, until golden brown, about 8 minutes.

Rub the toast with the halved garlic clove, and spread with your choice of topping.

CARROT BUTTER, WALNUTS, PIAVE CHEESE, AND HONEY

SERVES 4 TO 6

This carrot butter was a big hit at our table and truly couldn't be easier. One could take a similar approach with apples or pears. The result is a bright, beautiful spread that is smooth and just sweet enough—but much lighter than a real butter.

1½ cups water

½ teaspoon salt

½ teaspoon sugar

7 medium carrots, sliced into 1-inch-thick rounds

6 sprigs fresh thyme

¼ cup extra virgin olive oil

2 tablespoons honey, plus extra for drizzling

½ cup walnuts, chopped

¼ pound Piave or Parmesan cheese, shaved

Bring the water, salt, and sugar to a boil in a large saucepan. Add the carrots and thyme sprigs, and simmer until the carrots are tender, about 20 minutes.

Drain the carrots and discard the thyme sprigs. Transfer the carrots to a blender, and add the olive oil and honey. Puree until smooth, 3 to 5 minutes.

Toast the walnuts in a dry skillet over low-medium heat for about 5 minutes.

To serve, spread the carrot puree over each toast, and top with the toasted walnuts, shaved cheese, and a drizzle of honey.

WHITE BEAN, WARM RADICCHIO, CRISP BACON, AND SABA

SERVES 4 TO 6

One 15-ounce can white beans

8 tablespoons extra virgin olive oil, plus extra for drizzling

3 teaspoons fresh thyme leaves

½ teaspoon crushed red pepper flakes

1 clove garlic, finely chopped

1 bay leaf

Salt and freshly ground black pepper

1 head radicchio, sliced lengthwise into ½-inch wedges

1 tablespoon saba or a well-aged balsamic vinegar, plus extra for drizzling

½ teaspoon sugar in the raw

2 strips bacon, cut into 1-inch pieces

Drain the beans, reserving 1 cup of the liquid.

In a 2-quart saucepan, heat 5 tablespoons of the olive oil over medium-high heat. Add 2 teaspoons of the thyme leaves, the red pepper flakes, garlic, and bay leaf and cook, stirring occasionally, until golden brown, about 2 minutes. Add the beans, reserved bean liquid, and water to cover, and bring to a boil. Reduce the heat to medium-low and simmer until the flavors have melded, 10 minutes.

Discard the bay leaf and transfer the bean mixture to a blender; puree until smooth (sprinkle in a little water if the mixture is too dry). Season the puree with ¼ teaspoon salt and black pepper to taste. Transfer it to a bowl and set aside.

Heat the remaining 3 tablespoons oil in a 12-inch skillet over medium-high heat. Add the radicchio, and season with salt and pepper to taste. Add the saba and sugar and cook, stirring occasionally, until the radicchio is slightly wilted and caramelized, about 8 minutes. Set aside.

In a small skillet, fry the bacon pieces over medium-high heat until extra crispy. Remove with a slotted spoon and drain on paper towels.

To serve, spread the bean puree over each piece of toast, top with the radicchio and bacon, and sprinkle with the remaining teaspoon of thyme leaves. Drizzle with additional saba and olive oil.

HOMEMADE RICOTTA, WARM PEAR, AND THYME

SERVES 4 TO 6

1 tablespoon extra virgin
olive oil, plus extra for drizzling

1 Bartlett pear, sliced
(do not peel)

1 teaspoon coarse brown sugar

2 sprigs fresh thyme

1 cup homemade or store-bought
fresh ricotta (see page 234)

Sea salt to taste

In a small skillet, heat the olive oil over medium heat. Add the pear slices, brown sugar, and thyme sprigs. Cook for 3 to 5 minutes, until the pears are cooked but still retain their shape.

To serve, spread the ricotta over each toast, top with the pears, drizzle with olive oil, and sprinkle with sea salt.

HOMEMADE RICOTTA, SHAVED SQUASH, PARMESAN, AND LEMON

SERVES 4 TO 6

1 cup homemade or store-bought
fresh ricotta (see page 234)

1 small yellow squash, thinly sliced
on a mandoline

1 small zucchini, thinly sliced on a
mandoline

¼ cup fresh basil leaves, torn

Grated zest of 1 lemon

1 tablespoon extra virgin olive oil

Sea salt to taste

Spread the ricotta over each toast, and top with the yellow squash, zucchini, basil, and lemon zest. Drizzle with olive oil and top with sea salt.

COOK'S NOTE | *A great ricotta makes all the difference. Check with your local cheese shop or specialty market to find a homemade variety, or use our recipe on page 234.*

WHOLE ROASTED CAULIFLOWER

SERVES 6 TO 8

Roasting a whole cauliflower is a neat trick; it takes a bit of time but is well worth the endeavor. Get this one in the oven while you prepare the rest of the meal. The result is a mix of crispy exterior and tender interior—perfectly charred and well seasoned.

---

1 head cauliflower, outer leaves and core removed

¾ cup olive oil

½ teaspoon salt

½ teaspoon freshly ground black pepper

3 or 4 cloves garlic, smashed

2 lemons: 1 sliced, 1 juiced

3 to 5 sprigs fresh thyme

3 sprigs fresh oregano

Preheat the oven to 350°F.

Place the cauliflower right side up in a 9 × 12-inch baking pan. Drizzle the olive oil over the top of the cauliflower, allowing it to cover the entire head. The excess olive oil will pool at the bottom of the pan. Season the cauliflower with the salt and pepper. Scatter the garlic, lemon slices, and thyme and oregano sprigs around the cauliflower in the bottom of the pan.

Cover the pan with aluminum foil and roast for about 1 hour, until fork-tender, then remove the foil and continue to roast for another 40 minutes, until charred on the outside and soft on the inside.

Slice the cauliflower, and sprinkle with the lemon juice before serving.

MALTAGLIATI WITH WILD MUSHROOMS

SERVES 4 TO 6

The pressure of achieving a perfectly cut pasta is removed here—the beauty of this dish is in the imperfect hand-cut shapes. The pasta is topped with an array of roasted mushrooms, garlic, and herbs. In a pinch you could also break up store-bought lasagna noodles.

pasta dough

4¾ cups double zero ("00") flour, plus extra for dusting

7 eggs, at room temperature

¼ teaspoon salt

sauce

2 pounds mixed fresh mushrooms, cut into large chunks (we used cremini, brown beach, king trumpet, and oyster)

7 sprigs fresh thyme

2 tablespoons unsalted butter

3 cloves garlic, smashed and chopped

¼ cup olive oil

Salt and freshly ground black pepper to taste

1 tablespoon grated Parmesan cheese

Grated zest and juice of 1 lemon

2 tablespoons truffle oil

Make the dough: Mound the flour on a cutting board or in a bowl. Make a well in the center and crack the eggs into it. Sprinkle the salt around the edges of the flour.

Beat the eggs with a fork until smooth. Using the tips of your fingers, mix the eggs with the flour, incorporating a little at a time, until everything is combined. Knead the dough for about 5 minutes. Then form the dough into a disk and wrap it in plastic wrap. Allow it to rest in the refrigerator for 30 minutes.

While the dough is resting, make the sauce: Preheat the oven to 450°F.

Combine the mushrooms, thyme sprigs, butter, garlic, olive oil, and salt and pepper in a cast-iron or other oven-safe skillet, and roast in the oven for about 30 minutes. Keep warm.

Turn the dough out onto a floured cutting board. Cut it into 6 portions and roll them out into long oval shapes. Pass them through a pasta machine on each numeric setting to obtain thin sheets of pasta about 4 inches wide (the length can be as long you like). Cut the sheets into irregular shapes, such as triangles and rough trapezoids. Dust or brush the pasta with flour to prevent drying.

Bring a large pot of well-salted water to a boil, add the pasta, and cook for 2 to 3 minutes, until tender. Drain and return it to the pot. Pour the mushrooms over the pasta.

To serve, top with the Parmesan, lemon zest, and lemon juice. Drizzle with the truffle oil.

ICE CREAM SAMPLER

This dessert is a take on the beloved *affogato,* a traditional Italian dessert of espresso and gelato. Here we serve an array of flavors—some sour, some sweet—for a playful end to this meal. Add your favorite warm espresso on the side and enjoy.

PISTACHIO MINT ICE CREAM

SERVES 6 TO 8

2 cups unsalted shelled pistachios: 1 cup whole, 1 cup roasted and chopped for garnish

1 cup superfine sugar

½ cup fresh mint leaves

2 cups whole milk

2 cups heavy cream

12 large egg yolks

½ teaspoon almond extract

Combine the 1 cup whole pistachios and ½ cup of the sugar in a food processor and grind until fine, being careful not to turn the mixture into butter. Add the mint and grind a bit further. Set aside.

Bring the milk and cream to a boil in large heavy saucepan. Remove from the heat.

Combine the egg yolks and the remaining ½ cup sugar in a mixing bowl, and whisk to blend. Gradually whisk 1 cup of the hot milk mixture into the eggs. Then add the egg mixture in a slow, steady stream to the hot milk in the saucepan. Cook over low heat, stirring occasionally, until the custard thickens enough to coat the back of a spoon and reaches 170°F on an instant-read thermometer, about 6 minutes.

Remove from the heat and strain the custard into a large bowl. Add the pistachio mixture and almond extract. Cover with plastic wrap, pressing the plastic against the surface to keep a skin from forming, and chill in the refrigerator for at least 2 hours and up to 24 hours.

Pour the chilled custard into the bowl of an ice cream maker and freeze according to the manufacturer's instructions. When the ice cream is ready, transfer it to an airtight container and freeze until ready to serve.

To serve, garnish with the roasted pistachios.

SALTED CRÈME FRAÎCHE ICE CREAM

SERVES 6 TO 8

3 cups crème fraîche

3 cups whole milk

1½ cups superfine sugar

1½ teaspoons fleur de sel

15 large egg yolks

Pour the crème fraîche into a heatproof bowl and set aside.

Heat the milk, sugar, and fleur de sel in a large saucepan over medium-low heat. Do not allow the mixture to simmer or boil.

In a bowl, stir the egg yolks together. Gradually add some of the warmed milk to the yolks, stirring constantly as you pour. Pour the warmed yolks into the saucepan. Cook over low heat, stirring constantly and scraping the bottom of the pan with a heat-resistant spatula, until the custard thickens enough to coat the spatula. It will be about 180°F.

Strain the custard into the crème fraîche, and beat with a whisk to combine. Chill thoroughly; then freeze in an ice cream maker according to the manufacturer's instructions. When the ice cream is ready, transfer it to an airtight container and freeze until ready to serve.

BLUEBERRY AND BALSAMIC ICE CREAM

SERVES 6 TO 8

3 cups blueberries, fresh or frozen (if frozen, thaw and drain)

6 tablespoons balsamic vinegar

1 cup sugar, or more to taste

Pinch of salt

2¼ cups heavy cream

Combine the blueberries, vinegar, sugar, and salt in a medium saucepan and cook over medium heat, stirring, until the mixture boils and the berries pop and soften, 6 to 8 minutes.

Pour the berry mixture into a blender and blend until the puree seems homogeneous, about 1 minute (be careful when blending hot liquids). The mixture will not be completely smooth. Add the heavy cream and pulse to mix.

Pour the mixture into a bowl and refrigerate until thoroughly chilled. Then freeze in an ice cream maker according to the manufacturer's instructions. When the ice cream is ready, transfer it to an airtight container and freeze until ready to serve.

CHEESE TABLE

DRAWING INSPIRATION FROM THE SIMPLICITY of the Italian countryside, we spread out a canvas cloth and layer it with beautiful cheeses, olives, breads, and wines. This is a no-cook feast, one that can replace a meal or serve as a prelude to something grander. As guests trickle in, we mingle and chatter and drink loads of red wine.

At Sunday Suppers we often set out small bites for our guests as our way of warmly welcoming them into our space. When arranging this table, start with a layering of neutral linens, then add a few beautiful ceramics and boards: minimal design and high-quality ingredients.

CHEESE SELECTION

QUESO DE VALDEÓN
Blue; bold and spicy; pairs well with fruit

CHABICHOU
Goat's milk; creamy and fresh

OLD CHATHAM SHEEPHERDING COMPANY
KINDERHOOK CREEK
Pure sheep's milk; creamy with earthy mushroom notes

RICOTTA SALATA
*Pressed form of ricotta (literally means "salted ricotta");
firm, salty, and mild in flavor*

FIG LEAF–WRAPPED ROBIOLA
Artisan goat's and sheep's milk; creamy and delicate

OTHER BITS

OLIVES: GAETA AND CASTELVETRANO

BREAD: BAGUETTES

RAW HONEY

Purveyors at specialty shops and farmers' markets will often allow
you to taste cheeses before selecting them, and we highly encourage this.
Select a variety of textures and shapes and try to hit some of the key flavor
notes: Find an earthy sheep's milk cheese, a more delicate crowd-pleaser,
and a bold spunky one. Offer accoutrements that highlight these flavor
profiles and be sure to ask your cheesemonger for advice.

HOMEMADE RICOTTA

MAKES ABOUT 1 CUP

Homemade ricotta is creamy and lovely and one of the easiest recipes in our arsenal. We are lucky to have a few great neighborhood shops that offer their own versions of a homemade ricotta, but if you are in a bind or just feel like making a go of it, do—it is a showstopper.

4 cups whole milk

1 cup heavy cream

½ teaspoon salt

½ teaspoon sugar

Juice of 2 lemons

Line a large sieve with a layer of fine-mesh cheesecloth and place it over a large bowl.

Combine the milk, cream, salt, and sugar in a heavy 6-quart pot and bring to a boil over moderate heat, stirring occasionally to prevent scorching. Add the lemon juice and reduce the heat to low. Simmer, stirring constantly, until the mixture curdles, 2 to 4 minutes.

Pour the mixture into the lined sieve and let it drain for 1 hour.

Discard the liquid, transfer the ricotta to a jar, cover, and chill in the refrigerator; it will keep for up to 5 days.

THERE IS NOTHING QUITE LIKE a late summer evening on the beach. As the sun lowers and the cool air sets in, we inch a little closer to the warmth of the fire, where paella cooks over the flames. While we patiently tend to the paella, we serve crackers and marinated cheese. Charred tomatoes and beans, and warm olives scented with garlic and rosemary, fill the air with the loveliest aromas. We linger for hours, drink sangria, and enjoy one of the last nights of summer. As the sky darkens and the fire extinguishes, we head for home, merry and full.

MENU
SCALLOP AND SAUSAGE PAELLA

WARM OLIVES

MARINATED CHEESE

CHARRED TOMATOES AND BEANS

POMEGRANATE AND BLACKBERRY SANGRIA

CANELÉS

HOW TO BUILD A BEACH FIRE
Gather
BEACH STONES

DRY DRIFTWOOD OR FIREWOOD

Bring along
SHOVEL

MATCHES

METAL GRILL TOP (LARGE ENOUGH
TO COVER THE HOLE)

TONGS AND FORKS

BUCKET FOR CLEANUP

Dig a shallow hole in the sand, about 2 feet in diameter.
Line the hole with stones. Pile wood or found driftwood in the
stone-lined hole and light with a match. Place the grill on top.

Lopatin Residence
East Hampton, New York

SCALLOP AND SAUSAGE PAELLA

SERVES 8

Whether cooked over an open fire or indoors, paella is a welcome treat for guests. This version calls for sausage, scallops, and mushrooms, but one could certainly elaborate on or replace those items.

sofrito

2 cloves garlic

1 cup cilantro, including stems

½ onion, cut into 1-inch pieces

½ green bell pepper, chopped

⅓ cup olive oil

1½ pounds scallops

1½ pounds fresh chorizo sausage

2 pounds beech and cremini mushrooms

½ teaspoon salt

2 pinches saffron threads

2 cups dry white wine

3 medium vine-ripened tomatoes, seeded and cut into small cubes

4 cups chicken stock, plus extra

5 cups bomba rice

Aioli (recipe follows), for serving

Make the sofrito: Place the garlic, cilantro, onion, and bell pepper in a food processor and process until smooth.

Heat an 18½-inch paella pan over medium-high heat until it is hot. Add the olive oil, and sear the scallops for 2 minutes on each side or until golden brown. Transfer the scallops to a plate and keep warm.

Slice the sausage, add it to the paella pan, and brown until golden. Add the mushrooms and salt, and sear the mushrooms until golden brown. Add ¼ cup of the sofrito and cook for 1 minute without browning. Sprinkle in the saffron.

Add the white wine, and cook until it has reduced by three-fourths. Stir in the tomatoes and stock, bring to a boil, and cook for 2 minutes. Add the rice, spreading it evenly in the pan, and bring to a simmer. Do not stir the rice—if you do, the paella won't cook evenly. Reduce the heat and simmer for 10 minutes, adding more chicken stock if needed.

Top the paella with the warm scallops and remove from the heat. Allow it to rest for 5 minutes. Drizzle ¼ cup of the sofrito over the paella (refrigerate the rest) and serve with the Aioli.

AIOLI

MAKES 2 CUPS

4 cloves garlic

4 large egg yolks

Juice of 1 lemon, plus more to taste

1 teaspoon salt, plus more to taste

1 cup extra virgin olive oil

1 cup canola or grapeseed oil

Combine the garlic, egg yolks, lemon juice, and salt in a food processor and process until smooth, about 30 seconds. With the motor running, add both oils in a slow, steady stream. If the aioli becomes too thick, thin it with a tablespoon of water.

Adjust the seasoning as needed with more salt and/or lemon juice to taste.

WARM OLIVES

SERVES 4

A simple uplift to the standard olive plate, this warm appetizer works well before larger meals and at cheese gatherings.

1 cup Italian olives (gaeta or niçoise work well, or any of your favorites)

¼ cup extra virgin olive oil

1 sprig fresh rosemary

1 to 2 cloves garlic

Pinch of crushed red pepper flakes

Zest of 1 lemon, in strips

Combine the olives, oil, rosemary sprig, garlic, red pepper flakes, and lemon zest in a small saucepan, and cook over high heat until the mixture simmers, about 5 minutes. Serve warm, with bread or crackers.

MARINATED CHEESE

SERVES 4 TO 6

A few flavorings and some extra virgin olive oil combine to marinate a simple goat cheese for a wonderful spread. We like to pack this in a jar for picnics or backyard meals.

One 3-ounce log goat cheese, at room temperature

Grated zest of 1 lemon

2 bay leaves

Pinch of crushed red pepper flakes

¼ cup extra virgin olive oil

½ teaspoon flaky sea salt

Coarsely ground black pepper to taste

Place the cheese in a medium serving bowl, and top it with the lemon zest, bay leaves, red pepper flakes, olive oil, sea salt, and black pepper. Allow to marinate for 30 to 60 minutes before serving.

Serve at room temperature with crackers or crusty bread.

CHARRED TOMATOES AND BEANS

SERVES 4 TO 6

The simplest of dishes can often be the greatest, as seen here. Any summer produce would work in a similar manner over an open flame or roasted in a home oven.

2 pounds tomatoes on the vine

2 pounds green beans, trimmed

3 tablespoons olive oil

Flaky sea salt to taste

Preheat a grill to high or preheat the oven to 450°F.

In a bowl, coat the tomatoes and green beans with the olive oil. Place them directly on a grill grate or on a parchment-lined baking sheet. Cook for 5 to 10 minutes, until charred to your liking.

Place the tomatoes and beans in a serving bowl, season with sea salt, and serve.

POMEGRANATE AND BLACKBERRY SANGRIA

SERVES 6 TO 8

Spiked with pomegranate, this sangria is a bit of a change from the traditional wine punch. Prepare a batch a day ahead and serve it cold.

½ cup sugar, or more to taste

½ cup water

2 bottles Spanish red table wine

1 cup brandy

½ cup Triple Sec

1 cup orange juice

1 cup pomegranate juice

1 apple, sliced

Pomegranate seeds

½ cup blackberries

Make a simple syrup: Combine the sugar and water in a small saucepan, and heat until the sugar dissolves. Allow the syrup to cool completely.

In a pitcher or other container, mix the simple syrup with the wine, brandy, Triple Sec, orange and pomegranate juices, apple slices, pomegranate seeds, and blackberries. Seal tightly and refrigerate for at least 24 hours.

CANELÉS

MAKES 20 TO 24 PASTRIES

A specialty of Bordeaux, these pastries are custardy on the inside with a golden crunchy shell. Be mindful—one can easily eat too many!

1½ cups all-purpose flour

1½ cups sugar

2 whole eggs

2 egg yolks

¼ cup vanilla-infused bourbon

Pinch of salt

4 cups milk

4 tablespoons (½ stick) unsalted butter

Vegetable oil, for the molds

In a large bowl, combine the flour, sugar, whole eggs and yolks, bourbon, and salt.

In a small saucepan, gently warm the milk with the butter (remove from the heat before it bubbles). Add this to the flour mixture. Mix well, cover, and refrigerate overnight.

Preheat the oven to 425°F.

Remix the batter, scraping up the solids from the bottom of the bowl. Grease canelés molds (either copper or silicone) generously with vegetable oil and fill the cavities almost to the top with the batter. Bake for 50 minutes in copper molds or for 65 minutes in silicone molds, until the edges are quite dark.

Remove from the oven and let the pastries cool in the molds for 15 minutes. Then unmold and transfer to a wire rack to cool completely.

COOK'S NOTE | *If you'd like to get fancy with an even crunchier canelé exterior, brush your molds with a mixture of ½ stick beeswax and 3 tablespoons vegetable oil. (To make the mixture, simply warm the beeswax until it melts and then stir in the oil.)*

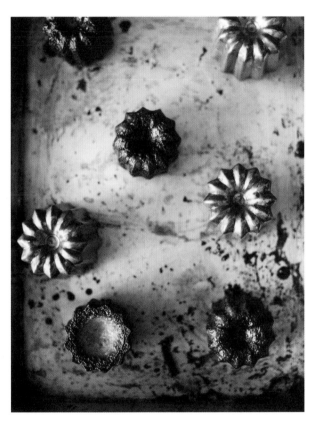

SOURCE GUIDE

Below is a list of go-to shops and retailers we use often when planning gatherings at home and for Sunday Suppers. If you are inspired to create a lovely meal in a beautiful setting, these resources will be helpful. You'll find that many of the grocery shops are local to New York, but I've also included many online resources that ship nationwide. I also urge you to seek out high-quality farms and producers in your own town and support them by buying their goods. You will find the most incredible gems.

GROCERIES + MARKETS

All Good Things
102 Franklin Street |
New York, NY
allgoodthingsny.com
212.966.3663

Blue Hill at Stone Barns
bluehillfarm.com

Chelsea Market
75 Ninth Avenue | New York, NY
chelseamarket.com
212.243.6005

Eataly
200 Fifth Avenue | New York, NY
eataly.com
212.229.2560

Essex Street Market
120 Essex Street | New York, NY
essexstreetmarket.com
212.312.3603

Good Eggs
goodeggs.com

McCarren Park Greenmarket
Union Avenue between Driggs
Avenue & North 12th Street |
Brooklyn, NY
grownyc.org
212.788.7476

New Amsterdam Market
902 Peck Slip | New York, NY
newamsterdammarket.org

Union Square Greenmarket
1 Union Square West |
New York, NY
grownyc.org
212.788.7476

Whole Foods
wholefoods.com

SPECIALTY GROCERS

Despaña Soho
Specialty Foods & Tapas Café
408 Broome Street |
New York, NY
despananyc.com
212.219.5050

Sweet Deliverance
sweetdeliverancenyc.com
347.415.2994

BUTCHERS

Fleisher's
fleishers.com
192 Fifth Avenue | Brooklyn, NY
718.398.MOOO

Marlow and Daughters
95 Broadway | Brooklyn, NY
marlowanddaughters.com
718.388.5700

Meat Hook
100 Frost Street | Brooklyn, NY
the-meathook.com
718.349.5033

SPECIALTY CHEESE + CHARCUTERIE

Bedford Cheese Shop
229 Bedford Avenue |
Brooklyn, NY
bedfordcheeseshop.com
718.599.7588

Cowgirl Creamery
Locations nationwide
cowgirlcreamery.com

Murray's Cheese
254 Bleecker Street |
New York, NY
murrayscheese.com
212.243.3289

SPECIALTY BREADS

Amy's Bread
amysbread.com

Balthazar
80 Spring Street | New York, NY
balthazarbakery.com
212.965.1785

Bien Cuit
120 Smith Street | Brooklyn, NY
biencuit.com
718.852.0200

Pain d'Avignon
120 Essex Street | New York, NY
paindavignon-nyc.com
212.673.4950

Sullivan Street Bakery
533 West 47th Street |
New York, NY
sullivanstreetbakery.com
212.265.5580

TABLEWARE + DECOR

ABC Home + Carpet
888 Broadway | New York, NY
abchome.com
212.473.3000

Alder + Co
537 SW 12th Avenue |
Portland, OR
alderandcoshop.com
503.224.1647

Anthropologie
anthropologie.com

Brook Farm General Store
75 South 6th Street |
Brooklyn, NY
brookfarmgeneralstore.com
718.388.8642

Canoe
1136 SW Alder | Portland, OR
canoeonline.net
503.889.8545

Canvas
199 Lafayette Street |
New York, NY
canvashomestore.com
212.461.1496

Fishs Eddy
889 Broadway at 19th Street |
New York, NY
fishseddy.com
212.420.9020

Fog Linen
5-35-1 Daita Setagaya |
Tokyo, Japan
foglinenwork.com
81.3.5432.5610

General Store
4035 Judah Street |
San Francisco, CA
415.682.0600
1801 Lincoln Boulevard |
Venice, CA
310.751.6393
shop-generalstore.com

Heath Ceramics
2900 18th Street |
San Francisco, CA
heathceramics.com
415.361.5552

Libeco
230 Fifth Avenue, Suite 1300 |
New York, NY
libeco.com
212.719.4646

March
3075 Sacramento Street |
San Francisco, CA
415.931.7433
marchsf.com

Mociun
224 Wythe Avenue | Brooklyn, NY
mociun.com
718.387.3731

Moon River Chattel
62 Grand Street | Brooklyn, NY
moonriverchattel.com
718.388.1121

The Primary Essentials
372 Atlantic Avenue | Brooklyn, NY
718.522.1804

Sur La Table
surlatable.com

Terrain
561 Post Road | East Westport, CT
shopterrain.com
203.226.2750

Union Made
493 Sanchez Street |
San Francisco, CA
unionmadegoods.com
415.861.3373

West Elm + West Elm Market
Stores nationwide
westelm.com

Williams Sonoma
williams-sonoma.com

DESIGN/TYPOGRAPHY/ CALLIGRAPHY

Erin Jang
New York, NY
theindigobunting.com

Knot + Bow
253 Third Ave | Brooklyn, NY
knotandbow.com
347.689.9818

Maybelle Imasa Stukuls
San Francisco, CA
may-belle.com
415.786.3515

Paperfinger
251 Washington Avenue,
Suite 2F | Brooklyn, NY
paperfinger.com

Simplesong Design
Washington, DC
simplesongdesign.com
703.679.8980

FLORISTS

Amy Merrick
amymerrick.com

Brittany Asch
brrch.com
845.323.7426

Fox Fodder Farm
foxfodderfarm.com

Saipua
147 Van Dyke Street |
Brooklyn, NY
saipua.com
718.624.2929

SPECIALTY ONLINE SHOPS

Analogue Life
2nd Floor | 4-9-2 Shogetsu Cho,
Mizuho-ku | Nagoya, Japan
analoguelife.com
81.052.933.7262

Herriott Grace
herriottgrace.com

Hudson Made
hudsonmadeny.com

Quitokeeto
quitokeeto.com

OTHER

Beekman 1802
210 Main Street |
Sharon Springs, NY
beekman1802.com
518.284-6039

Bellocq
Boutique tea house and atelier
104 West Street | Greenpoint, NY
bellocq.com
800.495.5416

Kate's Paperie
Paper goods + stationery
katespaperie.com

Kings County Distillery
Whiskey from New York City's
oldest whiskey distillery
63 Flushing Avenue, Building 121 |
New York, NY
kingscountydistillery.com
718.555.1212

Muji
Thoughtful selection of paper
goods and homewares
muji.us

Old Faithful Shop
320 West Cordova Street |
Vancouver, British Columbia
oldfaithfulshop.com
778.327.9376

Paper Presentation
Superstore for crafts and paper
goods
23 West 18th Street |
New York, NY
212.463.7035

THANK YOU

To the most important, wonderful, and gratifying little family a lady could hope for. To Ken for being my pillar and anchor and sometimes my compass in everything that comes our way. For letting me follow my dreams and my heart and for standing by me. To Sophia for being my light and my teacher in so many ways; I am honored to be your mother and I dedicate this book to you both. I look forward to a lifetime of cooking and meals ahead of us.

To the women in my life that I admire for their boundless assistance and inspiration. To Suann Song, whose capacity to give has taught me great lessons; thank you for the guidance and friendship. To Lizzy Sall for believing and contributing so much in those early days. To Marize Conradie for stepping into a wind gust with a calmness, a spirit, and a sweetness. To the women who inspire me every day to live what I do and do so with love. To my mother and grandmother, who taught me about food and family; I am so very grateful. And to my father, who has taught me strength, perseverance, and strength of character.

Thank you to those who opened their doors to host our gatherings for this book: Brenda and Jon, Katy and Nathan, Zach and Courtney, the Kings County Distillery. And to those who joined us at the table: Jen, Michael, Lauren, Lee Anne, Randi, Jacob, Marlow, Suann, Ike, Erin, Amy, Tommy, Yehuda, Malcom, Adam, and many more.

Thank you to Angelin Borsics who has been a believer and supporter in this book from day one, and to all the lovely people at Potter, including Ashley Phillips, Pam Krauss, and Doris Cooper. Thanks to Marysarah Quinn and Rae Ann Spitzenberger for your patience and calmness and for understanding my vision. And to Judy Linden, my agent and counsel who walked me through a new process and guided me at every turn.

To the crew on set and off who have helped at our suppers and book shoots. So many hands went into cooking, recipe testing and developing, propping and assisting. To all the interns, assistants, and friends who helped us cook and clean and open our doors to others.

And, of course, to all those who have dined at our table and supported us from the start. I am humbled and honored to thank everyone, sincerely.

INDEX

"*Karen Mordechai offers a gentle reminder to slow down and enjoy preparing simple meals to share with loved ones. You won't find trendy, complicated recipes in* Sunday Suppers—*her focus is on gathering around a communal table where good food leads to good conversation. From brunch to picnics to birthdays, Karen provides wholesome recipes that will nourish body and soul.*"

—NATHAN WILLIAMS, FOUNDING EDITOR OF *KINFOLK*

"*Sitting down to a meal with others is always an opportunity to learn, explore, ask questions, and expand one's worldview. It might mean meeting someone unexpected, or deepening existing friendships.* Sunday Suppers *celebrates the act of connecting over a shared meal. The recipes are gorgeous and the photography sublime. That said, the thing I love most is how Karen makes it all feel doable, and done beautifully, without a lot of fuss. Her menus are inspiring, the recipes accessible, seasonal, and crowd-pleasing—now it's time to daydream about the guest list.*"

—HEIDI SWANSON, AUTHOR OF
SUPER NATURAL EVERY DAY

"Sunday Suppers *is a beautiful meditation on the satisfaction of gathering—good food, friends and family, community—and sharing in the powerful experience of cooking and eating together.*"

—MELISSA HAMILTON AND CHRISTOPHER HIRSHEIMER,
AUTHORS OF *CANAL HOUSE COOKING*